᾿ ⸱᾿ ʋn Creel is a renowned psychic medium, with a broad
fan. se throughout the north-east of England. She has helped
ᴵ. ᴵ ᴵnds of clients find greater peace and healing. She has
⸱ ᵀ d all sorts of people – believers and non-believers – to
᾿ loved ones who have passed away. She believes anyone
lk to the spirits, provided they are willing to tap into their
ᵀc powers and practise using their intuition.

How to be Your Own Medium

Carolyn Creel

RIGHT WAY

For Geraldine. See, I told you it was real and now you know.

Constable & Robinson Ltd
55-56 Russell Square
London WC1B 4HP
www.constablerobinson.com

First published in the UK by Right Way,
an imprint of Constable & Robinson Ltd, 2013

A copy of the British Library Cataloguing in Publication
Data is available from the British Library

ISBN 978-1-8452-8516-6 (paperback)
ISBN 978-1-4721-1008-4 (ebook)

Printed and bound by
CPI Group (UK) Ltd, Croydon, CR0 4YY

1 3 5 7 9 10 8 6 4 2

Acknowledgements

I would like to thank the following people, without whom this book would never have come to fruition: Adam , your determination to make me succeed is inspiring and relentlesss in equal measures. From the bottom of my heart, I thank you for your constant support and searing honesty; Chloe, my shining light, you are indeed my reason for smiling every day; Susanna, you made what seemed like a difficult task surprisingly easy and pleasurable; and finally, to my mum and dad, thank you. I love you both.

Contents

Preface

Love never dies. It only changes. When a loved one passes over to the spirit world, their love transforms into energy. This book is about finding that energy, and using it to help you grieve and heal. It's also about helping you communicate with your loved one in spirit, in order to help you share messages of love and let go of negative emotions.

My name is Carolyn Creel, and I'm a psychic medium and counsellor. I'd like to offer you a warm and loving welcome to this book, and assure you that in these pages you will find support and friendship during what may be a difficult time.

In my work as a psychic medium, I have helped all sorts of people – believers and non-believers – talk to loved ones who have passed away. I contact the spirit world, and channel the spirits through me in order to share messages of love.

I believe anyone can talk to the spirits, if they are willing to practise their powers of intuition. By learning how to tap into your psychic powers, you can access the higher energy vibrations that come from the spirit world, and communicate with loved ones who have passed away.

Your departed loved ones are around you right now, providing loving energy.

In this book, you will discover that no matter what your background or beliefs, you can become your own medium. If you are prepared to practise and fine tune your psychic powers, you can use an amazing and ancient source of spiritual power that will ensure you are surrounded by love for the rest of your life.

I am going to show you how to communicate with departed loved ones, in order to find peace, heal, and move on with your life. Contrary to what some people think, communicating with the spirit world can help you through the difficult grieving process. Talking to a departed loved one in spirit can help you slowly but surely move on from loss, and become a stronger, more loving person.

When you communicate with the spirit world, you will discover that love is all around you. It never dies. It never disappears. It simply shows itself in different ways. You will learn that the spirits are always protecting you and sending you love.

Your departed loved ones are around you right now, providing loving energy. They are waiting and ready to connect with you. They may have even helped you to find this book.

Part I
Removing the Blocks that Prevent You Contacting the Spirit World

Chapter One

Thinking About Your Own Feelings

When someone dies, we tend to think a lot about them. Their last thoughts and wishes. Their manner of passing. Their funeral. The things they left behind. But I'd like to ask about you. How are you feeling? What's the day like for you, now your loved one is gone?

Do you have overwhelming feelings of sadness that aren't related to anything in particular? Do you sometimes feel angry, frustrated or upset over things that other people might consider small?

Negative, confused emotions are common when a loved one has passed away. However, they can block our communications with the spirit world. When we're not aware or accepting of our feelings, it makes it difficult to get in the right frame of mind to contact the spirits.

The good news is that, however you're feeling, you can connect with your loved ones in spirit.

If you were very close to your loved one, and their passing was recent, the chances are you're not feeling much like yourself right now. You may be feeling empty, angry, sad, deflated, lacking in energy, depressed or a combination of all these emotions and a few more besides.

If death was sudden, you may well still be experiencing feelings of shock, even months or years later. This is particularly true when younger people pass away. I often meet clients who tell me their world was turned upside-down one day, and they live their lives waiting for it to happen again. They can't rest or relax, for fear that something else bad will happen.

If you've had a few years to grieve, or your loved one wasn't part of your everyday life, you're perhaps feeling calmer and better. Thoughts of your loved one, while still sad, aren't quite so jarring. They're softer, and you're able to enjoy memories of them with fondness.

The good news is that, however you're feeling, you can connect with your loved ones in spirit. As long as you work to understand and accept your emotions, you can build a bridge to the spirit world.

In order to get in touch with departed relatives, it's important that your feelings and energy levels are beating at the right pace. We make this happen by recognising our feelings, accepting them and understanding them.

Let's find out a bit more about how you're feeling right now.

THE FEELINGS CHART

Below are five different categories of feelings. You've probably felt all of them at some point in your life, but what are you feeling most strongly right now? Read the categories below, and decide which two or three categories best suit your current feelings. You may be surprised.

Feelings of self

I feel like myself
I feel confident
I feel capable
I feel in charge of my life

Feelings of love

I feel loved
I feel safe
I feel protected
I feel cared for

Feelings of joy

I feel happy
I feel excited
I feel joyful
I am looking forward to the future

Feelings of sorrow

I feel sad
I feel depressed
I feel tired
I feel angry

Feelings of emptiness

I feel lonely
I feel empty
I feel there is nothing to look forward to
I feel I'll never get over this loss

Which feelings category were you drawn to? Was there one particular category that you felt represented how you're feeling right now?

It's important to understand your emotions, because contacting the spirit world is all about the emotional energy you're giving out. This 'emotional energy' can also be called your intuition.

The spirit world operates at a slightly higher vibrational energy than down here on earth, and in order to meet the spirits, we have to channel our psychic powers and intuition so our energy runs at a slightly higher vibration to match this. This means getting into a state of calmness that requires absolute emotional clarity. We must know what we're feeling and why. This doesn't mean we can't feel angry or sad. But we must acknowledge and accept these feelings, or our path to the spirit world may be blocked.

Were there any feelings in the Feelings Chart that came as a surprise to you? These are the feelings you most need to acknowledge and accept, in order to open your third eye, otherwise known as your intuition or subconscious. Once you're aware of all your feelings – good and bad – you'll have removed one of the major blocks to contacting the spirits.

A good way to discover hidden feelings is to take a pen and paper, and write a letter to yourself about how you're feeling. No one need ever read what you've written, so you can be completely honest. Ask yourself how you're feeling and answer as fully as you can.

Psychic Consultation

I've worked with a few clients whose strong emotions were blocking their ability to connect with the spirits. One of these clients was a lady called Marian, who'd lost her husband to a sudden heart attack.

On the surface, Marian felt nothing but love for her departed husband, but when I talked about how he passed away, I detected some anger that Marian hadn't yet dealt with. I asked her to go home and write a letter to herself about how she was feeling and *why* she was feeling that way.

When Marian came back to me, she seemed calmer and lighter. She told me that although she loved her husband very much, she was angry at him for the unhealthy lifestyle and stressful job that led to his death. In turn, she then felt guilty about this anger.

She had never truly acknowledged these feelings until she'd written the letter to herself, and when I reassured her that these negative feelings were perfectly normal, she was able to let go of guilt that she'd been carrying around since his death.

We were able to connect with her husband, and pass on loving messages from the spirit world. Marian felt reassured that her partner was watching over her, and that, with practice, she could connect with him herself, and receive messages of love as and when she needed them.

UNDERSTANDING HOW THE SPIRITS HELP SADNESS

People often come to me in a strong state of sadness. A loved one has passed away, and they're left feeling empty, alone and depressed. This is perfectly normal. The death of someone close is one of the most stressful experiences most of us will ever go through. It is okay to feel depressed and sad. It is normal to feel a sense of emptiness, and to be quite certain that life will never be bright, colourful or joyful again.

Most probably, you'll have heard that time heals all wounds. This is true, but when you're feeling wounded, it's hard to believe. When you're in a state of extreme sadness, all you know is how difficult it feels to live with these emotions.

Contacting your loved ones can help lift those feelings, if only for a short while, and give you a little breathing space. Grieving is a long and difficult process, and one for which there is no magic wand, but talking to your relatives in the spirit world will help you cope with feelings of sadness during the difficult years after a death.

Talking to the spirits will not take away the pain entirely, but they will help you grow as a person and heal. The spirits will also help you discover an abundant and eternal source of love that will help you work through your pain, and one day experience joy and happiness again.

BEING CLEAR ABOUT WHY YOU WANT TO CONNECT

In order to chart a clear path to the spirits, it's important to clarify exactly why you'd like to get in touch with your loved one.

I've met all sorts of people in my capacity as a psychic medium, and heard a thousand and one different reasons for wanting to contact the spirit world. Some people want to say goodbye. Others want to find out something they wish they'd learned while their loved one was still alive. Very commonly, people want to share or receive messages of love.

What's your reason for getting in touch with the spirit world? It's important you're very clear about your intentions. The lines between us and the spirit world are crackly at the best of times. If you are able to project a clear reason for getting in touch, you stand a greater chance of bringing the right spirit through, and communicating in the way you want.

So many people never get the chance to say goodbye to a loved one before they pass away. Sometimes this is because they are in a different town or country. In the very sad cases of a younger person dying, I often find the passing happens quickly and unexpectedly, leaving those left behind with so many unsaid words.

More commonly, though, people are near to a loved one when they pass away. They are at home, waiting for hospital visiting hours. Or walking the hospital grounds, while leaving a loved one to sleep.

So many people tell me there were things they wanted to tell their loved one before they passed away.

People seldom pass away when they are conscious and a loved one is present. I believe this is because we have a strong desire to hang on to life when a loved one is with us, even if the spirit world is calling very strongly.

This is the right and proper way of things, but for us – the ones left behind – it can be extremely painful not to have the chance to say goodbye.

So many people tell me there were things they wanted to tell their loved one before they passed away. Sometimes, this is quite simply these words:

I love you.

But sometimes there are other more complicated messages that people wish they could have shared. They worry that their loved one left this life without knowing something vitally important. Or they fear that their loved one isn't at peace, because the right words weren't said to them before they passed.

One of the reasons I enjoy my work as a medium so much is that I am able to put these fears and worries to rest. By contacting the spirit world and sending and receiving messages, I am able to reassure people that their loved one is happy and safe, and I am also able to communicate messages of love between this world and the next.

Let's talk now about your unique reasons for getting in touch with your relative. These are the reasons I hear most commonly:

I want to make sure my loved one is happy and at peace.

I want to know if my loved one is still with me and looking over me.

I never had a chance to say goodbye – I want to tell my loved one how much I care.

I want to make sure my loved one wasn't in any pain when he or she passed.

I want to find out if there is life after death.

I want to know if my loved one is angry or upset with me.

I would like forgiveness from my loved one.

Do any of these reasons ring true for you, or is there another reason why you'd like to make contact? You may well identify with several reasons on this list, and that's fine. Think carefully until you are absolutely clear about why you'd like to contact your loved one in spirit. Not only will clarity build a stronger path to the spirit world, it will also ensure you get all the answers you're looking for.

Chapter Two:

What Happens When We Die?

You may be surprised to find this chapter in the section about unblocking your psychic energy. However, I have found over the years that one of the biggest blocks to connecting with the spirits is fear or confusion over what happens when we die.

This fear may be subconscious, in that we never really realised we had it. Or we may have confused or mixed feelings about the afterlife, both in terms of what it means and how our loved ones are experiencing it. We may even be unsure if the afterlife exists at all, but simply hope that it does and that it's a happy place.

Some people visit mediums in the hope of finding out, one way or another, if the afterlife exists. They hope to hear messages from loved ones that demonstrate beyond doubt that the medium is in touch with a loved one in spirit.

I have certainly reassured people, on many occasions, that their loved one is still around and looking over them, and communicated messages that have helped people believe. I have met people who didn't believe in the afterlife, but were convinced after I've channelled for them.

However, I believe that when we seek proof, this can act as a block to contacting the spirit world. We have to contact the spirits with belief, and then they will show us the proof. If we approach the spirits with scepticism or doubt, it is much harder to create a clear channel.

BELIEVING IN THE AFTERLIFE

Do you believe in the afterlife? It's okay to have doubts, but if you have strong doubts, these will block your ability to connect with loved ones. Believing, on some level, that there is somewhere we go after we die is crucial if you're to get in touch with the spirit world.

If you have doubts about the afterlife, what are they and where do they stem from? Are your family and friends believers, or is the afterlife something they'd think was a little bit silly? Do you feel you need proof, before you can believe?

If you're not entirely convinced about life after death, let's talk through how beneficial it is to believe, and the real reasons behind your doubts.

> *We have to use our faith and listen to what our hearts tell us to be true.*

First and foremost, believing in the afterlife is a very great comfort to almost everybody. It reassures us that love never dies, but merely changes form. Believing in the spirit world helps us come to terms with the empty space in our lives that's left when a loved one departs, and to a certain extent helps us fill up that empty space and ease our suffering.

It has been proven that believing in an afterlife helps the living cope emotionally with death, and helps communities bond and heal.

We have doubts because we are afraid. We are afraid of looking or sounding silly. We are afraid of being made a fool of. We are afraid of wasting our time on something that isn't real. None of these fears is worth giving the time of day to.

In the world we live in, we place a very great emphasis on

science and proof. If we can measure and prove something, we accept it as real. If we cannot, we have a tendency to dismiss it. Until, of course, the time comes when we have the tools to measure it. Then even doubters would become believers.

We live in an age where we can't measure psychic energy, intuition or spiritual vibrations. One day, this will change. But right now, we have to use our faith and listen to what our hearts tell us to be true.

If you turn off the voices around you, the TV, the radio, newspaper reports, what does your heart tell you about where your departed loved ones are now? Do you feel they have simply melted away and gone out of existence? Or do you feel that, on some level, they are still with you?

I believe most of us know our loved ones are still with us in some form. Their loving energy is still close, even if their bodies are far away.

It's okay to have some doubts. You wouldn't be human if you didn't. But when it comes to connecting with the spirits, let go of your need for proof. Ignore anyone who says it's silly to want to believe in life after death.

When you contact the spirit world looking for proof, your vibrations are all wrong. You're bringing the low, heavy energy of logic and reason.

It's far better to focus on the positive feelings you have about the afterlife. We all have them, even the people who doubt the most. Think about the times you felt a closeness to the spirit world. When you experienced a feeling that there was an energy around you that wasn't from this world. Focus on your belief in the afterlife, not your disbelief, and you'll open yourself up to the spirits.

BEING AFRAID OF THE AFTERLIFE

A surprising amount of people are afraid of the afterlife, or at least certain aspects of it. This is especially true if people are part of a religion, or have been brought up in a religious family or community.

Religion can be a wonderful thing, but old-fashioned religious pictures of heaven and hell are sometimes a real hindrance to getting in touch with the spirit world.

For some people, even the words 'spirit world' can conjure up dark, frightening images and make them think of ghosts and ghouls. This is not helpful when it comes to contacting a loved one.

It's important to know that the afterlife is a happy, light and sunny place that matches the most positive experiences of a person when they were alive. It is a bright, loving place, full of kind and caring energy. It is a place where people transform into pure positive energy, and leave all their worries, aches and pains and problems behind.

Are you holding any fear when it comes to the afterlife? Let's see if we can find out. I want you to consider now where we go when we die. Try to use your feelings rather than your thoughts. Pictures and colours rather than words.

What do you feel when you think about the afterlife? Happy, calm, peaceful, excited or loved? Confused, afraid, lonely or sad?

What pictures come into your mind? Do you see happy images that make you feel good, or sad things that you'd rather not see?

What colours do you see? Light or shadows? Colours that make you feel happy and healthy, or colours that don't make you feel good?

Perhaps you see and feel a mixture of things, good and bad.

If your images of the afterlife aren't 100 per cent positive, I'd like you to change this right now. You're going to dream up a better, more loving and positive place for your loved ones to live – a place where their bodies are young and free, they have no problems and are surrounded by supporting, caring energy.

Find a restful space where you won't be interrupted. Take in three deep breaths, and let them out slowly. Now. Imagine the best place your loved one could possibly be. Imagine the surroundings they would like best. Imagine the sorts of people he or she would want to have around. Imagine him or her at their best – healthy and happy, laughing and having a great time.

This is where your loved one is now – or at least something close to it. Maybe they had different ideas than you about what they'd like to be surrounded by, but you can rest assured they are happy and at peace.

Psychic Consultation

A lady called Caroline came to see me, whose son had passed away at a very young age. She was, understandably, incredibly traumatised and upset by his sudden passing, and she was placing a negative focus on the way he'd been laid to rest. She'd wanted a cremation, but her husband had insisted on a burial. She was haunted by images of her young son being alone and cold in the ground, frightened and trapped in a wooden box.

I was able to reassure Caroline that her son had passed on to the spirit world, and was neither trapped nor alone. He was full of energy and leaping about when he came through, and I explained to her that he was surrounded by loving, caring souls who would look after him.

Although Caroline's grief was still considerable, she felt a great relief and lightness at hearing this news of her son, and was able to go about her life with more ease and comfort.

Caroline's negative pictures of the afterlife were completely understandable, but weren't doing her any good at all. It was a great relief for her to let them go, and if you have any negative pictures, I'd urge you to reconsider your ideas of the afterlife and paint yourself a more positive picture.

THE SPIRIT COMMUNITY

The afterlife isn't a place anyone goes to alone. When we die, someone always come to get us, and when we exist in the afterlife, we are surrounded by the spirits of departed loved ones and more loving energy besides.

No one need be afraid of dying, or that their loved one is in a bad place. The afterlife is a place of community and companionship.

To me, this is proved almost every time I do a psychic consultation, as the spirits are usually brought to me by the spirit of my grandfather. Because I'm close to my grandfather, I'm able to channel his spirit easily.

When contacting the spirits, it's always a good idea to have an open mind and entertain anyone who comes through.

You will find, as you tune into your own psychic energy, that people closest to you will come through most easily. This is why I believe that anyone can be their own medium. It is so much easier to channel spirits you are close to. Channelling spirits for other people is an altogether more challenging business, which will be covered in the later chapters of this book. However, channelling spirits you are close to is possible for everybody. It still takes practice, and I will share with you the techniques and disciplines you will need to get close.

The fact that my grandfather brings spirits through tells me that the spirits are all great friends. My grandfather's energy is always very loving and kind, and I know he is bringing other people through in a compassionate and caring way. I know he'd never bring through anyone who wasn't ready to talk, and I also know the spirits support and love each other in the afterlife.

When people don't understand how social and caring the afterlife is, this can be a further block to contacting the spirits. If you're only looking for one, specific person when you try to make contact, you can block the routes through which that person might come to you.

Often, people who have recently passed aren't ready to come through. However, 'older' spirits may help bring the 'younger' spirits through with them.

When contacting the spirits, it's always a good idea to have an open mind and entertain anyone who comes through. They may well have a link to the person you're trying to contact, and if you're not open to the bonds and links between spirits, you may well end up shutting out the very person you want to speak to.

Chapter Three:

Feelings About Your Loved One

If someone close to you passed away recently, you probably have *thoughts* about them all the time. These thoughts most likely pop into your head unprompted, and you may have them from the minute you wake up until you go to sleep at night.

Thoughts that come into your mind are not the same as feelings. Over time, thoughts fade but feelings grow stronger. It is your feelings you must focus on, and be clear about, in order to build a strong link to the spirit world.

When someone passes away, often our feelings about them are muddied. We go through such a range of emotions, from anger to guilt, fear, love and heartache, that it can be difficult to remember how we actually felt about our loved one. In this chapter, we will take some time to work through your feelings, in order to get your intuition in order and focus your psychic powers. We will also consider your reasons for contacting your loved one, to ensure clear focus and purpose when contacting the spirits.

For some, it can be too soon in the grieving process to attempt this sort of focus. That is perfectly understandable, and if your heart tells you it is too painful, feel free to leave this chapter for the time being.

THE DAYS BEFORE YOUR LOVED ONE PASSED

What were your feelings towards your loved one around the time he or she died? It is very common to have feelings that weren't altogether positive, either during or straight after a loved one's death. We often carry a lot of guilt about having these feelings, and this guilt can block our psychic energy.

It's important to acknowledge and work through these feelings, and to know that your loved one will accept and understand them. The afterlife is a place where all the silliness and pettiness of our world of possessions and physical bodies is forgotten. There is no pain or tiredness or stress. The spirits look down at us as pure energy, and can see right into our hearts. They know that all human beings think and feel negative things sometimes, but all is forgiven and understood.

I've talked to several people who have cared for loved ones through long-term illnesses, and found themselves feeling resentful and tired before a loved one passed away. Some people felt frustrated that a loved one wasn't taking their advice, or wouldn't commit to a healthier lifestyle.

I've also talked to people whose relatives were very depressed before they died, and weren't a lot of fun to be around. Other people have had loved ones who committed suicide, or died in accidents that could have been avoided. In these situations it's perfectly okay and natural to feel angry and frustrated. The spirits understand.

Spiritual Confession is a great way to clear any emotional blocks and make your peace with past negative feelings.

On the other hand, you may have had perfect, loving feelings before and during a loved one's passing. You may have been able to let go of frustrations, if indeed you had any at all, and felt nothing but love for the person who has passed over.

I'd like to take you back to just before your loved one passed away. How did the two of you get along? Were you in close contact? Was their death expected, and if so, have you been carrying around difficult feelings for a while? If their death was sudden, did you speak to them in the last few days before they died? Was your relationship in a 'normal' state, or were there things going on that were unusual?

Take a few deep breaths and remember. If it's too painful right now, that's okay. You can wait until a later time when you're feeling stronger. But if you're able, try to recall exactly how you and your loved one got along around the time they passed away.

I'd like you to take a pen and paper, and write down the negative things, if there are any. These might be things like: *didn't approve of his lifestyle,* or *blame her for the way she died and feel so angry.* I call this 'Spiritual Confession', and it's a great way to clear any emotional blocks and make your peace with past negative feelings.

Write whatever you felt (and maybe still do feel), knowing that every feeling is okay. In spirit, your loved ones don't seek out negative emotion and they won't mind what you write.

You may have nothing negative at all to write, and that is absolutely fine. Feel free to write feelings of love or sorrow instead.

If you did have negative feelings to express, you'll probably find you feel lighter after your confession. It's so easy to pretend there is no negativity surrounding the passing of your loved one, and that everything is loving and fine. But as human beings we have both light and dark sides, and it is very important to understand that it is okay to feel angry, guilty and frustrated sometimes – especially when it comes to death.

Since your intuition lives in your subconscious, it is very important to release any negative feelings you may have trapped there. You do this by being honest about your feelings, and accepting them.

HOW YOUR LOVED ONE PASSED

Sometimes, we can block our path to the spirits by getting caught up in how our loved one passed away. There are sometimes strong emotions relating to this, and they can cloud our memories and muddy our psychic connection.

If we feel a death is especially shocking, sudden or painful, our view of how a person passed on to the spirit world can be negative, and we find it hard to think of our loved one without pain and discomfort.

Often, spirits will tell me how they felt when they were last on the earth. They will tell me of stomach aches or sore heads or heart palpitations, and I will feel these pains in my body. However, in spirit people feel no pain. They are the very essence of energy, and exist only as love.

The truth is that passing away is a very gentle, loving and calm experience. The spirits have spoken to me about relatives coming to lead them to the next life, and how they felt calmness and love. Here on earth, we may be afraid of death, but for the spirits, there is nothing to be afraid of. No matter how sudden or unpleasant the circumstances of a death, the passing itself is a release from everything negative.

Sometimes, a manner of passing can be very shocking and upsetting.

It's important to acknowledge any negative feelings surrounding your loved one's manner of passing, and understand that they are not the same as the feelings we have for our loved one.

Fears, worries and trauma about a passing can block our path to the spirits, and get in the way of loving memories.

If your loved one died suddenly, it is extremely common to worry for other people close to you, and fear that they too will be taken away. Recognise any behaviours you have in this regard. Are you feeling more protective towards certain people? Understand that this behaviour, although positive in many ways, comes from fear, and that this fear has nothing to do with your real feelings towards your departed loved one.

Sometimes, a manner of passing can be very shocking and upsetting. If a loved one was involved in an accident, there can be all sorts of unresolved feelings. Anger at others who survived or caused the accident is very common, as is anger at your loved one if you feel carelessness was to blame. The feeling that a death could have been prevented, or indeed that you personally could have done something to prevent a death, can be one of the most difficult and debilitating emotions to carry around.

If your departed loved one was a parent, it's common to worry that their manner of passing will be your own. I've often spoken to people who changed their diet or lifestyle as a result of a parent passing away. It's surprising how often people aren't consciously aware they are doing this, but all of a sudden quit smoking or take up exercise after a passing.

It's great to take positive action after a tragedy, but it's also important to acknowledge and accept the fear that created this action. If you've changed your lifestyle after a parent has passed, recognise that this may be in direct response to fear – your very rational fear of dying.

Consider all the feelings you have about how your loved one

passed away. Recognise that they are not the same as the feelings you have for your loved one. Accept that it is okay to have these feelings, but recognise them for what they are and know where they came from.

Guilt, anger, blame and hatred are all part of human nature. They are part of us. As long as we accept them, we keep our third eye open.

One day you will be able to let go of the negative feelings surrounding a difficult passing. The spirits don't want us to feel any negative emotions – especially guilt. They are at peace and happy, and want only the same for us.

SPENDING TIME WITH YOUR LOVED ONE

When someone passes away, it's natural to think about them obsessively. They enter our dreams, and are our first thoughts on waking. They sneak into our thoughts at every moment during the day, and all sorts of everyday activities remind us of them.

Often these thoughts bring sadness and tears, especially in the early days. Many of us get used to suppressing thoughts of our loved ones, for fear of breaking down in public. We learn to control our thoughts and hold back the tears.

It's no bad thing to take charge of your thoughts, but it's also important to give yourself space to explore *feelings* about your loved one in a healthy way at a time of your choosing. You can think of this as spending time with your loved one, and easing them out of your life.

Death – especially if it's sudden – often brings overwhelming feelings of emptiness. If your loved one's life was very entwined with your own, you have to adapt both to death, and to huge changes in your lifestyle. This can be very difficult when you have so many emotions running around. Good feelings about your loved one can be a real comfort, and a way to make life a little easier.

One of the easiest ways to 'spend time' with your loved one is to visit a quiet place that was special to them. Visit this place at a time when you won't be rushed, and turn off mobile phones and other distractions. You don't need photographs or any visual reminders – you're trying to tap into the feelings, not thoughts.

Take as long as you like to be with your loved one. Talk to them. Tell them how you're feeling, and imagine they're right beside you, giving you comfort.

Psychic Consultation

A lady came to me in a terrible state after her husband had passed away. He'd visited a GP the day before he'd died, but a serious condition had gone undiagnosed. It was only when he was rushed to hospital that evening that medical staff realised how ill he was.

The next day he passed away suddenly, and it was the last thing this lady was expecting. Her husband had been on the verge of retirement, and they were planning a long and happy old age together.

She had overwhelming feelings of anger towards the doctor who'd failed to diagnose her husband, and was pursuing a vendetta against him. This was consuming her life in a very unhealthy way. She believed the doctor had ruined her last memories of her husband, as she had such negative emotions surrounding his passing.

We talked through the way she was feeling, and she was able to separate her feelings of anger from the loving feelings she had towards her husband.

I contacted her husband in spirit, and he was calm and at peace, and wanted his wife to feel the same. Although she couldn't immediately let go of her anger towards the doctor, she was able to understand that the anger was very different from her feelings about her partner. She left feeling calmer than she had in a long time.

Chapter Four:

Connecting with Your Intuition

We all have intuition. In fact, it's one of the human race's most magical and amazing gifts, and yet most people don't use it – or at least, not very often. For many of us, when we do use our intuition, it's an afterthought. Logic and reasoning come first, and only then do we listen to our gut feelings.

Intuition opens up new worlds of understanding, and can bless us with incredible knowledge and wisdom. It is the gift that makes us appear 'psychic', as we 'know' things without being directly told. Used in the right way, intuition can bring true balance to our lives and give us astonishing insight.

I find it amazing that we're all blessed with such an amazing gift, yet so few of us use it regularly. But then again, the world we live in has a tendency to scoff at this gift, so I suppose it stands to reason that we let our intuition take a back seat.

In order to build a clear path to the spirits, you need to be best friends with your intuition. You need to remove any blocks that stop you tuning in to your intuition. Don't worry – it's easy to strengthen your intuitive feelings once you start practising, and I'm going to show you how.

WHAT IS INTUITION?

Most of us have an understanding of intuition, but let's really firm up what I'm talking about.

Intuition is known as many things – gut feeling, instinct, psychic energy, the subconscious mind, inner wisdom, first reaction…and I'm sure you've felt it many times in the past. Whether you listened to it or not is a different story.

Have you ever walked into a house, and had a bad feeling about it? That's your intuition. Have you ever known who was calling before you picked up the phone? Intuition again. Your gut feeling can talk to you about incredibly simple, everyday things, like which vegetables to buy or which side of the street to walk on. It can also help you with major life events like where to live and whom to marry.

> *Logic says 'I know'. Intuition says 'I somehow know'.*
> *You don't need proof when your intuition knows something –*
> *just listen to it!*

Intuition comes from the gut and your emotional centre, rather than your head. When your intuition talks to you, it shares feelings first, thoughts second. It usually starts with a feeling in your stomach or chest. The trick is to let that feeling work its way up to your head, and listen to the messages it is telling you.

Intuition is lightning fast – you can know something in a millisecond that your logical mind will take months to work out. An amazing tool, don't you think?

Logic says 'I know'. Intuition says 'I somehow know'. You don't need proof when your intuition knows something – just listen to it!

How many times have you had a gut feeling about something, not listened to it, then thought to yourself 'I *knew* that would happen…I wish I'd listened to my gut'?

When you start trusting your intuition, one of the biggest blocks to the spirit realm will be lifted.

HOW WE BLOCK OUR INTUITION

We all have very strong and powerful intuition. The skill is in listening to it. Now, this isn't always easy – especially if your intuition is telling you something you don't want to know. This can be particularly true around issues of ill health and lost loved ones. But I'm here to tell you that intuition will be your best friend, once you get used to listening to it. It will protect you and take care of you, while logic can often give you the wrong advice.

However, there are ways we all block our intuitive feelings. Even those of you who already have a good relationship with your intuition will block your feelings sometimes. It's a perfectly normal and natural thing to do in a world that celebrates logic and science above all things.

Let me tell you the key blocks that stop us listening to our intuitive feelings.

Pain

Pain in the body and the mind can be a great block for the intuition. Why? Because when we're not feeling good, we try to block out everything – good and bad. We distract ourselves with television or overwork, and try to distance ourselves from life with things like alcohol.

It's perfectly understandable that when you're in pain, you want to try and shut out life, or distract yourself. But it's important to understand that once you start shutting things out, you're also disconnecting yourself from your intuition.

A good way to embrace pain, and your intuition, is to be alone.

If you're in pain – either because you're grieving, or because of something in your body – you have two choices. You can either wait until the pain has gone, or eased. Or you can let the pain come, and with it your intuition.

We're often very frightened of pain, and we live in an age that tells us there's always something to shut pain down or turn it off. But once you embrace it and try to accept it, you'll find it isn't as frightening or as bad as you thought.

A good way to embrace pain, and your intuition, is to be alone. No distractions, no alcohol or medication that will take you away from life – just you and your thoughts, feelings and pain. Experience what needs to be experienced, and listen to any wisdom from your intuition that comes along the way.

Ego

Ego is the part of you that wants more, more, more. More money, more success, more power. It sees you as separate from everyone else, judges people and puts everyone into boxes.

The real you knows that, deep down, all human beings are the same. We're all loving, caring creatures who share the same sun and would sacrifice our own needs to help others. But we all have moments when the ego takes over.

> *Thinking of other people instantly moves you out of an ego state, and into a loving, intuitive one.*

The ego values you first, and everyone else second. When we're in times of pain, the ego often rears its ugly head. We can feel so caught up in grief that we forget about everyone else, and that's perfectly natural and normal. But remember when you're in a 'me, me, me' frame of mind, connecting with intuition is difficult. Intuition is the real you. The kind, genuine you that loves and cares.

Here's a very simple way to move away from the ego, especially if you're grieving. Go help someone else. Perhaps you can message a friend who's also lost someone, or give your loved one's possessions to someone who needs them. Voluntary work is good too. Even if you're feeling low on energy, you'll find uncanny reserves when it comes to helping others.

Thinking of other people instantly moves you out of an ego state, and into a loving, intuitive one.

Fear

Sometimes, we're afraid of what our intuition will tell us. After all, what if it's bad? Or what if it's something we've hidden from ourselves for good reason? This is especially true for people who've had traumatic things happen to them in the past.

I find meditation is very helpful in creating a calm state of mind and reducing anxiety.

While these fears can be well justified, you should know that fear itself is worse than any messages your intuition has for you. Your intuition is always loving and kind, and has your best interests at heart.

I often find that people who visit mediums do so because they're afraid of their own minds. They'd prefer someone else tuned in for them.

How do you overcome fear of your intuitive thoughts and subconscious mind? I find meditation is very helpful in creating a calm state of mind and reducing anxiety. If you've never been before, attend a local meditation session, or download a meditation class online. Once you've experienced clearing your mind in a peaceful, calm way, you'll find you're a lot less afraid of hearing messages from your intuitive self.

Psychic Consultation

A beautiful young girl called Natalie came to see me after the loss of her brother. She was extremely close to him, and his sudden death came out of the blue and turned her world upside down. He'd left behind a young wife and child, and Natalie was finding it very hard to understand how life could be so cruel.

Although Natalie wanted to connect to her brother, she was afraid. What if he was in pain? What if he was in a dark place or unhappy? Or what if he just wasn't there anymore? She sensed he was still around her, but was scared to listen to those 'other-worldly' voices in case they told her something bad.

I was able to reassure her that her brother was happy and at peace, and that he didn't remember anything of his passing. I was also able to help her open up to the voices she was hearing. After listening to her brother through me, she understood that spirit messages from loved ones are always good and kind.

Shock

When something traumatic happens, we often go into a state of shock and disbelief. This is particularly true when it comes to death, since the loss of a loved one is one of the most traumatic things that will ever happen to us.

I often have clients tell me that they lived in a state of shock for weeks after a loved one died. Sometimes even months and years – especially if a death came out of the blue.

When you're in shock, hours become seconds and great sections of your life go missing. You know a week has passed, but you can barely remember what happened.

Shock isn't something to be hurried out of. It will pass when it passes. Give yourself as long as you need to heal and make sense of this new world, and only begin connecting with loved ones when you're ready.

LEARNING TO TRUST YOUR INTUITION

Think about what might be blocking your intuition. Do any of the above blocks apply to you? If so, take some time to work through them before you start attempting to connect with your instincts.

If you're feeling unblocked and ready to tune in, then let me help you learn to trust and listen to your instincts. You're about to welcome an ancient and astonishing source of power into your life, and you'll soon wonder how you ever lived without its wisdom and advice.

> *While you're connected with your intuition, the spirits will be very close to you.*

Let me show you an exercise I use almost every day to connect with my intuition and psychic energy. It's very simple, but very powerful.

Connecting with Your Intuition Exercise

Find a comfortable place where you feel at ease and at peace. This could be somewhere in your home or garden, or another place — perhaps a favourite library or park. You'll need about ten or fifteen minutes the first time you do this exercise, but as you get better, you'll be able to connect much quicker. These days, I can connect in three minutes or less.

Take a seat and place both feet firmly on the floor.

Relax and take seven deep breaths, breathing in through the nose and out through the mouth. While you're doing this, imagine a ball of light at your feet. As you're breathing, picture that ball of light moving up through your legs, up through your stomach, heart, throat and crown until your whole body is filled with white light.

Allow the white light to move up and down through your body until you feel totally, utterly flooded in white light.

Now, let questions come into your body. What do you want to know? What do you want answers to? Those answers will come to you, often as feelings rather than words.

In this state of relaxation and light, you're connecting with your intuition or higher self.

While you're connected with your higher self, the spirits will be very close to you. They'll be trying very hard to communicate, and as long as you're open to them, you may just hear them — even at this early stage.

The more you exercise your instincts and listen to your intuitive self, the easier it will be to connect.

One of the best ways to open up the channels is simply to talk to the spirits, just as you would anyone else. You don't have to talk out loud. Just start a conversation in your head. I like to say hello and welcome any spirits who may be around, and tell them that I'm open to what they have to say.

You'll probably find that once you open up the channels, all sorts of strange words and thoughts will pop into your head – that's the spirits talking!

EXERCISING YOUR INTUITION

Intuition is like a muscle. The more you exercise it, the stronger it gets. But of course, you have to know the muscle is there to start exercising it! The more you exercise your instincts and listen to your intuitive self, the easier it will be to connect.

I'm going to share a great exercise for strengthening your intuition. If you do this every day, I guarantee that within a few months your intuition will be as strong as many professional psychics!

Free Flow Exercise

This exercise is so simple, but really, really effective. Before you go to bed tonight, I'd like you to put a pen and large notebook under your pillow.

When you wake up the next morning, write down the first thoughts that come into your mind. Don't censor them or think too hard – just write whatever words, thoughts and feelings come. They don't have to make sense. Just write!

Keep going until you've filled a whole A4 page, or the equivalent.

The things you write can be totally mundane and boring. You're not trying to be Shakespeare, just noting down what's flowing around your head.

You'll be amazed at how your life will change for the better once you start listening to your intuition.

This free flow exercise does two things.

First, it clears out any excess logic that is clogging your intuitive knowledge. Now, I'm not saying there's anything wrong with logic, but too much of anything is a bad thing, and in the world today, most of us have too much logic flowing around.

Second – and most importantly – it taps into any free-flowing, intuitive thoughts. You'll recognise them instantly. They're the thoughts that just *make sense*, and feel both brand new and years old.

The more you do this exercise, the more intuitive thoughts you'll write down, and the more able you'll be to recognise them.

You'll be amazed at how your life will change for the better once you start listening to your intuition. You'll experience the kindness, loving energy and wisdom that comes from your own soul. Better still, you'll be well on your way to removing emotional blocks to the spirit world, and tuning in to departed loved ones.

And of course, the more you're aware of your intuition, the more you'll use it. The more you use it, the stronger it will become. Just knowing how important it is to listen to your gut will open you up to a tremendous source of universal wisdom and loving advice that will strengthen and guide you.

Chapter Five:
Using Dreams to Hear
Your Psychic Self

Dreams are a great link to the subconscious and our intuition. When we sleep, our mind automatically relaxes and goes into a calm state, creating a natural gateway to the intuition and psychic self.

Even those who have a great deal of trouble hearing their intuitive self while they are awake will have no trouble while they are sleeping.

Once you understand how the psychic self talks to you through dreams, you will be able to hear your intuition more often while you're awake. As you start recording your dreams and really focusing on the messages they contain, you will understand how your intuition works and strengthen your link to it.

WHY DREAMS ARE THE GATEWAY

While we are awake, our mind is constantly on the go. It is assessing, judging, remembering and learning. Most of us rarely use our intuitive mind during waking hours. Instead, we let logic run the show.

I believe that we should use our intuitive mind just as much as our logical mind. However, because we live in a logical world, most of us aren't practised at keeping our mind in balance. Indeed, most of us can't even recognise the difference between intuitive thinking and logical thinking. This is where dreams can help.

When we sleep, our mind works in a completely different way than when we are awake. It relaxes and slows down. All the things we learned with our logical mind are sorted and placed into the subconscious.

> *Because the intuition is creative and not logical, it likes to use symbols and word play to get its message across.*

Sleep is where our intuitive, creative self takes over. All the things we experienced during the daytime are assessed by the intuitive side of our mind.

Logic is thrown to one side, and our intuition gets to think over what the day's events meant. The intuitive mind may interpret things very differently to the logical mind. For example, if you went to a job interview and thought it didn't go very well, your intuitive mind may have picked up all sorts of positive signals that say the complete opposite. You may then dream about a job interview situation, or similar, that goes extremely well. This is your intuition trying to help you understand the day's events from another perspective.

I believe that because we are so out of balance these days, and use our logical minds far too much, we dream more than we should. Having nightly colourful dreams is a sure sign that your intuition is desperate to share things with you that it wanted to say in the daytime.

Dreams can be extremely useful, both in hearing your intuitive self, and in understanding how the intuition communicates. Because the intuition is creative and not logical, it likes to use symbols and word play to get its message across. Once you understand how the intuition shares messages, you will be much more able to hear these messages during your waking hours.

SEEING THE DEPARTED IN DREAMS

Because we are in a relaxed and meditative state when we dream, we are in exactly the frame of mind needed to link to the spirits. The key to connecting with the spirits is to calm the mind and let go of everyday concerns. Because we do this automatically in sleep, almost everyone will have had spirits visit them in dreams. However, when the departed show themselves in dreams, it can feel quite random and out of your control. This book is about taking charge of the psychic connection and making contact as and when you choose.

The spirits always show up as their best self, because this is how they are now they have passed.

When you see the departed in dreams, they will always look healthy and happy. If they were ill before they passed, you will see no signs of this. They will be fit and well, and in the prime of their life. When you start making daytime connections with the spirit world, you may see images of your departed loved one too, and these images will also be of fit, healthy and happy people. The spirits always show up as their best self, because this is how they are now they have passed.

Seeing the spirits in dreams should go some way to helping you understand that you do have psychic abilities, and really are able to connect to the spirit world. After all, if you can do it while you're asleep, it can't be so difficult to do it in your waking hours!

Because in the early days you won't be able to control when the spirits come to you in dreams, there may be times when you wish that they wouldn't. In this case, before you go to sleep, simply tell the spirits that you don't wish to see them and they won't come.

HOW INTUITION TALKS TO US IN DREAMS

Dreams are about more than seeing the spirits. They are truly the voice of our intuitive self, and our intuitive self has plenty to tell us about all sorts of things.

The more you understand the messages from your dreams, the stronger the link to your intuition will be, and the more you'll hear messages in your waking hours.

The key to understanding your dreams is to work on feelings, not logic. How did your dream make you feel? When did you last feel that way in your waking hours?

Let me give you an example. Imagine you were driving home from work and a small child ran out in front of your car. You slam on the brakes and just miss the child, but of course you still feel frightened, shaken up and a little guilty if you weren't paying attention to the road.

That night you dream that you're in a forest cutting down a tree. Just as the tree is about to fall, you see a nest of baby birds up in the branches. You hold the tree firm to stop it falling and shout for help. As the tree topples this way and that you feel frightened, and as it comes crashing to the ground you feel very shaken and shocked. Fortunately the little birds are okay, but you still feel guilty at having cut down their home.

> *The more you focus on feelings in dreams, and mapping where*
> *and when they came from in waking life, the more you will*
> *understand your intuition.*

Do you see how the feelings in this dream link to the feelings you had in the daytime? Once you've linked the feelings, you can then understand other links. For example, the baby birds represent the child in the road.

Dreams are all about *feelings*. No matter how weird and wonderful and strange your dreams appear, if you work out how they made you *feel*, you can almost always link them to something that happened in the last few days.

The more you focus on feelings in dreams, and mapping where and when they came from in waking life, the more you will understand your intuition. Focusing on your feelings in this way will help you understand your mind much better. You'll start to listen to your gut instinct more, and understand what your feelings are telling you. This in turn will help your intuition speak to you during the daytime.

If you don't dream very often (or even not at all), this suggests you have a strong link to your intuition and listen to your gut feelings regularly during the daytime. However, you can still choose to hear your intuition through your dreams if you wish, and see the spirits while you are sleeping. Before you go to sleep, tell your mind that you'd like to dream tonight, and most likely you will. It's as simple as that!

RECORDING YOUR DREAMS

The trouble with dreams is that they're like cobwebs. Just the tiniest of breezes will blow them away. Most of us dream every night, and yet we only remember a handful of dreams over a life-time – and even then in very little detail.

The more you record and pay attention to your dreams, the stronger the link will be to your intuitive mind.

To strengthen your understanding of your intuition and how it talks to you in dreams, you need to record your dreams as soon as you wake – even if that's in the middle of the night. Keep a pen and paper, or Dictaphone, beside your bed and write down or record every detail of a dream as soon as you can. Even as you write or record, you'll find details of the dream slipping away – so work quickly! Focus on your feelings first. Did you feel frightened, happy, nostalgic, angry? Feelings are the most important thing to record. Now jot down all the little details. The colours of things, the 'storyline' to your dream. Because dreams like to talk in symbols, make particular note of animals, water (including rivers and oceans), travel (running, driving, etc.) and falling, as these can often point to very important messages.

The best time to interpret your dream is as soon as you wake. This is when your memory will be clearest and your logical mind at its quietest. Ask yourself, what is this dream trying to tell you?

The more you record and pay attention to your dreams, the stronger the link will be to your intuitive mind. This link will build without you having to try too hard, and you will soon find that listening to intuitive feelings during the daytime is much easier.

TAKING CONTROL OF YOUR DREAMS

The more you pay attention to your dreams, and build a link to your intuition, the more control you will have over your sleeping thoughts. As time goes on, you may well find yourself experiencing something called 'lucid dreaming', which is a sort of cross between a meditative waking state and dreaming.

You'll see all the vivid images of dreams, but you will have some control over what you're seeing and hearing. It's a strange state, and hard to explain unless you've been in it, but it usually comes about just before you're about to wake. It's somewhere between sleeping and waking, but it's also very close to the relaxed state we try to put ourselves into when we make contact with the spirits.

For this reason, a lucid dream is an excellent opportunity to make contact with departed loved ones. All you have to do is tell your mind to bring your departed forwards and, more likely than not, your loved one will walk right into your dream.

You can then ask questions, just as you would if you'd made a daytime connection. You can also hug your loved one and tell them how much you miss them.

Until you're very experienced, lucid dreaming is a state that's tricky to bring about. You can certainly ask your mind, before you sleep, to bring you a lucid dream, and you might be lucky enough to get one. But generally, they come when they come, and if you experience one in the early days of improving your psychic abilities, you're very lucky indeed.

The more you focus on and record your dreams, the more likely you are to have a lucid one.

Psychic Consultation

A gentleman called John came to see me after the passing of his mother. He was living in her old home, and dreamed of her often. John enjoyed seeing his mother in his dreams, especially since she always looked happy and healthy. She cracked jokes too and was very cheerful, just like when she was alive and well.

In John's dreams, his mother was often cleaning up after him and telling him what to do with the house. She kept telling him to get his own place, and that a man of his age shouldn't be living with his mother.

John was worried that dreaming about his mother so much was a little unhealthy, and that it had something to do with living in her home. He asked me if perhaps he should move house, so he could put her memory to rest.

It seemed to me that John's intuition was telling him exactly that. It was time to move on. His dreams were saying that he was living in his mother's home, not his own, and that it was time to branch out and start a new, more independent life.

John agreed with this interpretation, and said that although he loved seeing his mother while he was asleep, he felt that he'd never move on with his life if she kept visiting. I suggested that he simply ask his mother not to visit so often, which he did.

When I saw John again, he'd moved house and was much happier. He still liked to see his mother in his dreams occasionally, but he saved this for special occasions like her birthday. He really felt he had control over his dreams now, and could pick and choose when his mother's spirit came through.

Chapter Six:

Exploring Doubt and Disbelief

It's okay to have doubts about the afterlife. But you have to understand that these doubts can become a real block between you and the spirits if you don't recognise and understand them.

This chapter is all about working through doubts and disbelief, so you can build a clear path to the spirits. You don't have to get rid of your doubts entirely, but you do have to notice them, then learn to put them to one side when you're trying to connect with loved ones.

WHY DO WE DOUBT?

Many people these days say they don't believe in the spirit realm. It's not fashionable to say that you believe in anything you can't see, and many people seem to think it's okay to laugh at people who claim to talk to the spirits.

> *I promise that by the time you've finished reading, you'll have some sort of spiritual experience with a loved one who has passed.*

There's nothing wrong with a bit of healthy scepticism. After all, there are plenty of con artists out there waiting to take advantage of people who are grieving. But there's nothing wrong with belief either. In fact, belief is what gets us through life. And it's what makes miracles happen.

Let's focus on you for a moment. I'm guessing you have some belief in life after death otherwise you wouldn't be reading this book. But you may also have some doubts. You may even be reading this book as a way to find proof about the spirit world.

I promise that by the time you've finished reading, you'll have some sort of spiritual experience with a loved one who has passed. But not until all your emotional blocks are removed, and these include your doubts.

Here are some common doubts about life after death, and my thoughts on how to deal with them. Are any of these *your* doubts?

It's not scientifically possible for the spirit to exist outside of the body.
Isn't it? Our life essence is nothing more than energy. Just like electricity, that energy can be stored in different places. Energy doesn't die, it just moves around. We don't have a way of measuring souls or spirits right now, but I believe that one day we will.

I've been to a séance or medium, and they got everything wrong.
Yes, I'm sad to say some experiences with mediums don't turn out well. Not all mediums truly tune in to their intuition. Instead, they rely on parlour tricks. I've seen some truly awful mediums at work, but I've also seen some amazing ones. It can be the luck of the draw. The good news is that when you learn how to connect personally with your departed loved ones, you'll be your own medium. And who better to trust than yourself?

I want to believe, but I just don't feel anything when I think about the spirit world.
That's because you're too tuned in to your logical mind, and

not connected to your intuition. Over-thinking is a very common problem in this day and age, and something you will work through during the course of this book. Once you start connecting with your intuition, you'll start feeling the spirit world.

Surely if the spirit world truly existed, there would be some concrete proof?
My own experience is proof to me that the spirit world exists. As your intuition grows stronger, you'll see and hear proof of the spirits all the time, just as I do.

However, the spirit world can't be measured with scientific tools. The energy of spirit is all about feelings, and in this age of logic we don't have many tools for measuring the more intuitive side of life.

Even the most sophisticated brain-scanning machine can't measure subtle emotions like joy, relief, guilt and contentment. Amazing, isn't it? We can send men and women to the moon, but we still can't measure feelings.

My family and friends would laugh at me if they knew I was trying to contact the spirits. Surely if so many people doubt, they have to be right?
I completely understand this doubt. Working as a medium means I come across my fair share of cynics and sceptics, and they can be pretty cruel, let me tell you. I've never doubted the existence of the spirits, so I don't mind if others choose not to believe. I'm happy to laugh along when people make fun of the afterlife, because I feel that I'm happier and healthier for my beliefs.

However, there is a real power in numbers. If all the people around you choose not to believe, this can make you doubt. After all, if your close friends and family suddenly swore that the sky was red, you might start thinking...*is it?*

I find the easiest way to overcome this doubt is simply not to share your interest in the spirits with doubters – even if those doubters are very close to you. Keep your interests to yourself, and you'll avoid cynical comments and doubts being thrown your way.

Now let's consider your own personal doubts are about the afterlife, and work out where these doubts come from. Nine times out of ten, our doubts don't come from us at all, but from other people.

Take a pen and paper, and write down five doubts about the afterlife. Don't think too much, just write. Now. Where did these doubts come from? Can you trace them back to their roots?

Psychic Consultation

A lady called Rita came to see me after her husband had passed away. She really wanted to make contact, but she was finding it difficult to overcome her doubts. She came to me asking for proof that her husband really was out there.

I told her that as long as she was holding on to doubts, it would be difficult to make contact. Doubt operates at a low energy level, whereas the spirit world operates at a higher vibration. As long as Rita was doubting, I knew I would struggle to make contact.

I decided to analyse Rita's doubts, and really get to the bottom of where they came from. Rita's main doubt was a practical one. She just couldn't picture a place where all those spirits would live. How could there be space for them all?

Together, we worked out that this doubt came from her father, who was a sceptical man. He would sneer at the idea of heaven and hell, and say that with all the millions of people in the world, it wasn't possible for them all to hang around.

I helped Rita to picture the spirit world – a place of infinite space, where the human personality existed in a totally different way.

Now she had somewhere to 'put' her husband's spirit, her doubts faded away, and we were able to make contact very quickly. Rita cried tears of joy when her husband came through, and she was able to leave my session in a lighter, more loving frame of mind.

THE DOUBT TEST

How strong are your doubts? Here is a simple test to see where you are on the doubting scale. If you carry a lot of doubt, don't worry. I have an exercise to help let go of disbelief. And during the course of this book, you'll find that your doubts diminish. The more you work with your intuition and feelings, the fewer doubts you'll have.

I'd like you to answer true or false to the following questions. Sounds easy, but actually the questions are designed to make true or false answers difficult! So what I'd like you to do is give the first answer that pops into your head. Don't think too much – just decide straight away.

True or False?
Part I
1. I believe in the afterlife.
2. I feel the spirits of loved ones around me.
3. My departed loved ones talk to me.
4. I know my loved one hasn't truly gone.
5. Love never dies.

Part II
1. I'm afraid of dying.
2. I don't have a clear picture of the spirit world.
3. Death means emptiness and endings.

4. I need proof before I believe.
5. I'm afraid of trying to connect with a loved one, and not hearing anything.

I'm hoping that for Part I of the test, you answered mostly true, and for Part II you answered mostly false. However, if you gave three or more 'false' answers in Part I, and/or three or more 'true' answers in Part II, we need to do some work on your doubt and disbelief.

If the test showed that you do have a lot of doubt, please don't worry. The purpose of this section is to help you work through any blocks between you and the spirit world. We have to *find* those blocks before we can remove them. Finding the blocks is half the battle.

So what should you do if you have doubt? Well, reading this book is a great start. But right now, I have a powerful visualisation exercise that has helped many of my clients put their doubts to one side.

Giving the Spirits a Home Exercise

This exercise is all about picturing the afterlife. When you create a clear image of where your loved ones are, you'll find many of your doubts about life after death miraculously disappear. This is an excellent exercise for helping you believe, and strengthening your intuition.

You can be as cynical as you like about this exercise. I've seen the biggest doubters become the biggest believers once they create a clear picture of the afterlife. So feel free to doubt!

To carry out this exercise, I'd like you to go somewhere you feel the spirit of a departed loved one.

This can be a church, graveyard, bedroom, duck pond
– even a football stadium. You might choose a place
where ashes were scattered, or just somewhere your
loved one liked to be.

Remember that the afterlife is a warm, loving and caring place.

Take ten deep breaths, breathing in through your
nose and out through your mouth. Feel a ball of white
energy in your feet. Let that energy travel up through
your body until it's washing up and down, flooding
you in white light.

    Now I'd like you to picture the afterlife in as much
detail as possible. Let go of practicalities and reach
out with your feelings. What do you see, feel and
hear? Endless green meadows? A blue sky? Let your
imagination have fun, and fill in as many details as you
can. What do the spirits look like? What are they doing?

    Take at least twenty minutes to picture the
afterlife. Remember that it's a warm, loving and
caring place.

HOW COINCIDENCES HELP YOU BELIEVE

We've all experienced coincidences when it comes to departed loved ones. By coincidences, I mean those magical things that make you feel your loved one is near, just when you're thinking about them or really needing a pick-me-up.

Think now about any coincidences that told you your loved one was nearby.

I remember one of my clients telling me her departed brother loved butterflies. When she scattered his ashes, three butterflies came to land on the grass nearby, and one landed on the urn.

Another client sold his departed girlfriend's car, which she loved, just before the funeral. On the day of the funeral, he saw the car being driven a few cars ahead of the hearse. The person who bought it had nothing to do with the family and no idea the funeral was on that day.

Coincidences are proof that your loved one is nearby, and they can really help you let go of any doubts and disbelief. The trick is to both remember and value coincidences. Far too many of us just let coincidences slip by without paying attention to them. If we do pay attention, we dismiss them as 'just a coincidence'.

Think now about any coincidences that told you your loved one was nearby. Allow yourself to really value that coincidence, and use it to help you feel the energy of your loved one.

THE BIGGEST DOUBT OF ALL...

What's the biggest doubt of all? Needing to *see* before you believe. Whenever I hear clients say this, I explain that they have it the wrong way around. They need to believe before they can see. And 'see' won't be in the usual sense, either. When it comes to the spirits, 'seeing' really means 'feeling'.

Once you start focusing on your feelings, you'll be much closer to the spirits and much freer of doubts. And once you let go of your need to see proof, you'll be well on your way to communicating with your departed loved one.

Chapter Seven:

Believing in Your Own Abilities

Most clients come to me because they believe I have a gift that they don't possess. When I tell them that I believe everyone is psychic, they often look at me in wonder. 'Really?' they say. 'You think everyone is psychic? Even me?'

The answer is yes. Everyone is psychic. The key difference between me and someone who isn't a medium is our belief in our psychic abilities. Now, of course, another difference is that I've practised my intuitive abilities for many years. But I'd never have practised those abilities if I hadn't believed that I had a psychic gift in the first place.

So this chapter is all about helping you believe in your psychic powers. Because until you truly believe, your way to the spirits will be blocked.

I'm going to share with you some stories and mantras to help you believe in yourself, and hopefully by the end of the chapter you'll feel a much stronger sense of your psychic powers and the possibility of connecting with the spirit realm.

WHY DON'T WE BELIEVE IN OURSELVES?

I find that the main reason we don't believe in our psychic abilities is because intuition and life's 'softer' skills aren't encouraged in this day and age. Most children who have psychic experiences don't tell people about them, for fear of being mocked, laughed at or called a liar.

Psychic experiences are usually dismissed as coincidences or imagination. We're not taught to practise our psychic skills – far from it. In life, we're told to focus on 'practical' and 'sensible' things like mathematics and English language. There are no lessons at school about feelings or tapping into intuition.

I'm willing to bet that you've had more than one psychic experience in your life. Perhaps you didn't call it a psychic experience, but you understood that it meant there was something more to the world than you could see with your own eyes.

When I was a young girl, I used to wake up and see my granddad sitting at the end of the bed. This wouldn't be strange, if it weren't for the fact that my granddad had passed away. Of course, at first I didn't realise I was having a psychic experience. I thought I was seeing the end of a dream, or just having a hallucination.

Now I understand that Granddad's spirit was coming to visit me, and of course these days I see him all the time. He's the spirit who comes through first, when I connect with the spirit realm, and helps me find whoever I'm looking for.

> *If we'd been taught to notice our own psychic abilities from a young age, I believe we'd all be professional mediums by adulthood.*

I've heard many stories from clients about experiences they've had with departed loved ones. These experiences are commonly straight after a passing, when our psychic senses are heightened and our logical mind takes a break.

I remember one lady telling me she saw her husband on an empty hospital bed, a few hours after he'd passed away. She'd come to collect his belongings, and wasn't startled or surprised to see him sitting there, propped against the pillows. Instead, she felt totally calm.

Her husband was smiling and looked healthier than she'd seen him in years. He blew her a kiss, then disappeared.

Afterwards, the lady decided that she'd simply had a hallucination due to shock. During our consultation, I asked her to really focus on this memory. When she recalled it in detail, she understood she'd connected with her husband's spirit that day. She'd never hallucinated before in her life, and her feelings of peace and calm actually came from the connection she had made with the spirit realm.

Because we don't learn about intuition at school, and because we're not taught to focus on the 'invisible' side of life, we don't tend to recognise it. If we'd been taught to notice our own psychic abilities from a young age, I believe we'd all be professional mediums by adulthood.

YOUR PSYCHIC EXPERIENCES SO FAR

I'd like now to consider the psychic experiences you've already had. Focusing on coincidences, visions, psychic dreams and when you just 'knew' things will really help you believe in your own psychic powers.

So let's take a trip down memory lane. I'd particularly like to focus on the time after you lost a loved one, because this is often when our psychic energies are most in tune.

When your loved one passed away, were there any strange coincidences surrounding their death? Perhaps something happened with their possessions that you weren't expecting, or perhaps you ended up hearing their favourite song while you were thinking of them, quite by accident. Maybe you saw or felt their presence, or had a very vivid dream about them that told you something very important.

Whatever your experiences, I'd like you to really focus on them. Find a quiet spot and really relive the memory in detail. What were you wearing? What was the temperature? What exactly did you see, hear and feel?

The more you focus on this experience, the more you'll begin to value it as a genuine psychic encounter. This will help you appreciate that you *do* have psychic powers and you *can* connect with the spirit realm. You just need to believe and start practising.

Psychic Consultation

A gentleman came to see me after the loss of his son. He was absolutely distraught, as you can imagine, especially since the death was very sudden. He was desperate to connect with his son, and told me he'd prayed many times that his son would come through and let him know he was okay.

During the session, my grandfather came to me and brought with him a handsome little lad riding a bright red bicycle. The boy was the gentleman's son. He was happy and content in the afterlife, riding his favourite bike and playing with the family dog who had passed over some years previously.

When I told the gentleman about my vision, he looked at me in alarm. He told me that a few weeks ago, while he was praying for his son's spirit to come through and talk to him, he'd had a vision of him riding his red bike.

My client had been lying in his bed, staring at the ceiling, when he saw his son very clearly, riding a bicycle and waving, with a big smile on his face.

I was happy to tell this man that he'd had his own psychic vision of his son and, if he chose to, he could develop his own abilities and see his son whenever he liked.

The man was astounded and pleased to realise that he possessed these abilities himself. He told me that before our visit, he would never have realised the 'vision' of his son was real. But now he understood that he too could connect to the spirit world. All it took was for him to believe.

HOW WORDS LEAD TO FEELINGS

Have you noticed how words can have a big effect on your feelings? For example, how do you feel when you see this word?

DEVIL.

Personally, I feel a little afraid. Like most of us, I've grown up with all sorts of awful pictures of hell and damnation, and I see the word 'devil' as something very frightening and unpleasant.

Now let's try another one.

ANGEL.

Better? I like this word too. Who doesn't? It brings to mind a lovely, kind, light energy, doesn't it?

The words we use in our lives have tremendous power over us. Your feelings are strongly linked to the words floating around your mind. If those words are positive and full of belief, you'll find it much easier to achieve your goals.

Now. Take a look at this sentence.

'I don't really believe I have psychic powers.'

How does that sentence make you feel? Do you agree with it? Perhaps it makes you feel annoyed, because you do believe you have psychic powers. Or perhaps it worries you because you'd like to have psychic powers, but aren't sure you really do.

How do you think you'd feel if you had that sentence floating around your mind, and you said it to yourself every day? Do you think you'd find it easy to connect with the spirits, or very difficult?

> *I know mantras can feel a little silly, but I promise you they're extremely powerful.*

I believe that many people do have that exact sentence lodged in their mind. They tell themselves often, without even realising it, that they don't have any psychic abilities. Can you imagine anything worse for your self-belief?

The good news is, you can decide which words you'd like to let into your life. And better still, if you select powerful, positive words, they can make a really big difference to your self-belief. So let's try something better:

'I am psychic.'

How do those words make you feel? Could you say them out loud without feeling embarrassed or dishonest?

The best thing about words is that even if you don't believe them, the more you let them into your heart and mind, the more they have an effect. You don't even need to do anything to make them true. Just say them often enough, and your mind will start to understand that they *are* true.

So let's try those words again.

'I am psychic.'

And here are some more sentences to try:

'I have psychic powers.'

'I am powerfully intuitive.'

'I am able to receive messages from the spirit realm.'

Sentences like these are called 'mantras' and it's been proven that saying mantras regularly is an extremely powerful way to change your thinking and give yourself new confidence and abilities.

I'd like you to choose one of the above sentences and say it to yourself every morning, as soon as you wake up. If you can, say it out loud, looking at yourself in the mirror to really power up what you are saying.

I know mantras can feel a little silly, but I promise you they're extremely powerful. If you choose a 'psychic' mantra to say every morning, I know that after a few weeks you will have a much stronger belief in your psychic abilities.

Part II
Talking to Loved Ones

Chapter Eight:

Are You Ready for This?

Now that we've worked on your emotional blocks, it's time to prepare for contact with the spirit world. It's important that your reasons for contacting the spirits are the right ones, and that you're not looking for an escape route from grief.

If you've lost a loved one recently, you may well not be feeling like yourself at all. This is an incredibly difficult time emotionally, and it's only natural to want an escape from negative feelings. However, I'm sorry to say that the spirits can't take away pain. They can only soften it and give you comfort and company.

You need to understand exactly what the spirits can and can't offer you, before you make contact. You also need to accept that connecting with the afterlife may not turn out exactly as you planned – but this doesn't have to be a bad thing.

ARE YOU LOOKING TO ESCAPE GRIEF?

I often ask my clients why they want to get in touch with the spirit world – especially if I sense they may not be in the right frame of mind. I listen carefully to their reasons, and then together we decide if communicating with the spirits is the healthiest thing to do at this time.

Quite often, when someone has lost someone recently, they are looking for a way to end their pain and grief. They are finding life unbearable, and believe that the spirits may offer some sort of pain relief or bandage for their suffering.

I always tell recently bereaved clients that the spirits can only give so much. Grief is a long and painful process, and something we must go through in order to heal. There is no escape route or quick path through it, and the spirits won't take our grief away.

What the spirits *can* do is help with feelings of guilt, loneliness and anxiety. When we know that our loved ones are close by, we don't feel so lonely or isolated. We also don't feel that we're 'being a bit mad' by talking to them or feeling their presence.

> *When clients are suffering from extreme grief, I work hard to help them understand exactly what they can expect from the spirit world.*

The spirits can put any guilty feelings to rest too, and let us know that we did everything we could for our loved ones while they were alive. They can alleviate our anxiety about the way they passed, letting us know that they felt no pain and are now at peace. They can also help us with our own fears of death, since once we feel our loved ones are around in spirit, we know we'll go to a loving place when we pass.

If you're looking to make contact with a loved one to end the grieving process, I'm very sorry to tell you that the spirits can't do that. Grieving takes time. If you make contact as a way to end your pain, the chances are you'll be very disappointed.

When clients are suffering from extreme grief, I work hard to help them understand exactly what they can expect from the spirit world. I strongly believe that if you try to make contact during the early stages of grief, you must be aware that the spirits may not offer everything you would like. Sometimes, it is best to wait until you are in a healthier, happier place before you make contact.

MY THREE 'MAKING CONTACT' QUESTIONS

Let me take you through the three questions I ask clients before we try to make contact with the spirits. These questions will help you work out whether now is the best time for you to communicate with the spirits, or whether you're better off waiting until your feelings are a little less raw.

How would you feel if you couldn't make contact?
Sometimes, with the best will in the world, you won't be able to contact your loved one in spirit. You'll either draw a complete blank, or end up talking to another family member who has passed. How would you feel about that? If you'd feel desperately disappointed, heartbroken, rejected, lonely or frustrated, then perhaps it would be best to wait a few weeks or months before trying to make contact.

The spirit world operates at a high vibration of energy, and low, negative energies like frustration can block your path to it. Feeling desperate to get in touch, or placing a lot of pressure on the need to make contact, is a great way to block your way.

Let some time pass and wait until you're feeling calm, loving and in control.

What if you made contact, but your loved one doesn't say what you expect?
In spirit, we have different concerns and values. We no longer have a human body, and time is meaningless. We don't share the same concerns we had on earth, and so the things we choose to share with our loved ones may not be what is expected.

Spirits often tell me seemingly mundane or trivial things, which are their way of proving that they're watching over us and seeing everything we do, no matter how 'unimportant'.

Sometimes, clients get frustrated when spirits won't talk about 'big life events'. But to the spirits, every detail is important. You can't force the spirits to talk about anything they don't want to. You're the receiver. You just have to listen and receive what they want to tell you.

How would you feel if the messages you received weren't the ones you were looking for? If you'd feel deeply frustrated, angry or disappointed, it may be a good idea to wait awhile before trying to make contact.

Do you have someone with whom you can share your experiences of making contact?
Communicating with a loved one in spirit can be a real head spinner. You'll probably experience a whole range of emotions, and think about what was shared for weeks to come. It's important that you have someone with whom you can share your experiences – someone supportive, who is accepting of the spirit realm. Ideally, this person will be a close friend or relative, and someone who will listen and let you share your feelings.

THE 'RIGHT FRAME OF MIND' CHECKLIST

There are some key thoughts and attitudes you should have before trying to make contact with the spirit world. I have a 'right frame of mind' checklist that I use to help clients decide whether they're truly ready to meet the spirits.

Look at the questions below and answer yes or no.

Are you happy to accept that your loved one may not come through when you try to make contact?

Are you willing to listen to and accept whatever your loved one has to say?

Are you open to all spirits, not just one?

Are you able to feel calm about the idea of contacting the spirits?

Do you have at least one friend or relative who accepts that you want to make contact, and will let you talk about your experience?

If you can say yes to all or most of the above, then you are probably ready to make contact. However, only you know for certain. What does your heart tell you? If you truly feel you're ready, and you're not looking for an escape route from grief, then let's begin our journey into the world of spirit.

Chapter Nine:

Calming Down and Tuning In

When people ask me what skills are needed to be a psychic or medium, I always say that being able to feel calm is probably the most important one. Why? Because it's from a place of calmness and stillness that we make our connection with the spirit realm.

Only when our mind has stopped chattering away can we truly listen to our intuition and feelings, and understand messages from the spirits.

Being able to feel calm is a skill, and it's something that you can and should practise. You'll find that once you've learned how to calm yourself down, it will help you in all areas of your life.

A calm mind is the very foundation of contact with the spirit world. Without a sense of calmness, the whole connection will be wobbly and fall down. But when we're in a place of stillness and peace, our connection with the spirit world is stable and messages come through loud and clear.

THE BEST BREATHING

Calmness always starts with breathing. The simple act of controlling our breathing and bringing more air into our bodies will instantly release feelings of calm. With practice, you can help this calm spread all around your body and hold onto it for as long as is needed.

Usually, our breathing matches how we're feeling. When we're tired, we breathe more slowly and calmly. When we're frightened, our breathing gets quicker and higher up in our chest. When we're really scared, we breathe very quickly in short little breaths, and don't take any air deep down into our lungs.

Taking control of your breathing is the first step to becoming calm.

How do you breathe when you're feeling calm? Deep and slow, taking air right down into the bottom of your lungs and your abdomen.

Take a breath now and let it go right down into your abdomen, so your belly area rises and falls. Can you feel how breathing all the way down your body like this instantly makes you feel calmer?

Taking control of your breathing is the first step to becoming calm. When you start telling your body to feel calm by breathing slowly, your mind will follow. How soon it will follow depends on, you've guessed it – practice!

Let's practise breathing for calmness right now. Read this next section through once before trying the exercise.

One Minute Calm Exercise

This is a great exercise for feeling calm quickly. You can use it almost anywhere, although I wouldn't recommend it while you're driving as it can make you feel drowsy.

The more you practise this exercise, the more your body will accept calmness as your permanent state of being.

I'd like you now to take long, slow deep breaths, breathing all the way down to the bottom of your lungs and into your abdomen. Breathe in through your nose and out through your mouth.

As you inhale, count slowly to seven. Now hold the breath for a count of four, and let out the breath slowly to a count of seven.

Take three breaths like this, counting to seven and holding for a count of four.

Now you're going to take seven breaths without holding for a count of four. Breathe in to a slow count of seven and out to a slow count of seven.

You'll find your body relaxing with every breath you take. Your mind will feel still and clear, and your body soft and comfortable.

PLACES OF CALM

You may have noticed that some places have a calm feeling to them. These are almost always spiritual places, like churches, mosques and Buddhist centres. As humans, we're attracted to these places to celebrate the lives of our lost loved ones. We understand that they have a special energy about them that in some way helps us feel connected with the departed.

You can use the energy of these places to help you feel calm and centred. When you visit spiritual places, notice how you're feeling and bring the energy of calm into your body. You may even like to use places of calm to make contact with the spirits.

CALMING CANDLELIGHT

Candles have long been used in séances and other spiritual gatherings. As humans, we understand that firelight has a very special power, especially in making us feel calm and putting us in the right emotional state to meet the spirits.

If you don't have any candles in the house, I'd urge you to go out and buy some simple heavy-based white candles, turn off the lights and sit in the candlelight. Focusing on the flickering and dancing of a flame is a wonderful way to switch off from the logical mind, and the dim lighting will help you relax and stay calm.

FRUSTRATION – THE ENEMY OF CALM

Calmness is not a state that can be forced. You have to relax into it and let it come. The more frustrated you feel, the harder it will be to feel calm. And the more you try to grab hold of calm, the more slippery it will be. Hold onto calm lightly and it will stay with you.

> *Frustration is the enemy of calm, and calm is what's needed to contact the spirits!*

I often find clients get a little frustrated when we're trying to make contact with the spirit world. Because it's not something in their control, they feel a sense of powerlessness – especially if we struggle to connect.

I always say that this feeling of frustration is often the exact reason that making a connection is difficult. Frustration is the enemy of calm, and calm is what's needed to contact the spirits!

If you experience frustration when you're trying to feel calm, I have a simple task that will help you practise letting go. The next time you have a free morning, get on the first bus you see and let it take you where it takes you. Don't look at the destination on the front of the bus – just see where you end up.

The aim of this task is to let life take control of you for a change. You'll find everything turns out just fine – and you might find some really interesting things on your journey.

WHEN FEELING CALM IS DIFFICULT

For some of us, feeling calm is more difficult. If you have a challenging job or little time to yourself, you may well be in a real state of stress that is difficult to snap out of. If you're in a stressed state, and you've lost someone recently, you may feel calm is impossible. With all the emotions swirling around, coupled with the pressures of life, you may be holding so much tension in your body that breathing alone doesn't bring you to a calm state.

If the breathing exercise above did little for you, or if you snapped right out of your calm state almost as soon as you were in it, we need to work a little harder to make you feel relaxed.

No matter how busy your life is, I believe you can make time for meditation.

I'd like you to start meditation sessions. Meditation basically means sitting in silence, and letting all thoughts fade away. You can take part in guided sessions, where an experienced practitioner will help you calm your mind and reduce your stresses. Look on the internet for meditation centres near you.

If getting to a meditation session is difficult, you can download guided meditations from the internet and listen to them three or four times a week.

I personally feel that going along to a meditation session is better than listening to a recording alone, as you have the collective calmness of the group to keep your mind in check. However, downloadable meditations are still good, and a great substitute if you can't make a class.

No matter how busy your life is, I believe you can make time for meditation – especially if you're in a stressed state. Ask others to help you if needs be. Taking this time will truly help you, not just in connecting with the spirits, but in all aspects of your life.

CALMNESS IN GRIEF

You might be surprised to learn that when you're grieving, calmness can come even more easily than usual. We experience such a turmoil of emotions when we lose someone close, that you may feel calmness is very far away. But I promise you, it's exactly because of these supercharged feelings and heightened emotions that we can enter an extremely calm state while we're grieving.

When you have lost someone, suddenly all those silly little details of life no longer matter.

The logical mind takes a back seat when we lose someone close to us, and emotions take over. This means that as long as we can quieten these emotions, we are in the perfect state to feel calmness in the mind. There will be no logical thoughts to distract us once we quieten our emotions. The usual trivial, domestic thoughts that bother many people don't bother those who are grieving.

When you have lost someone, suddenly all those silly little details of life no longer matter. You only care about the important things, and truly the only important thing is love.

When you're grieving, you will need to place your focus on calming your *emotions*, rather than your *thoughts*. This can be done by tuning in to your body and working out which emotions you're feeling and where you're holding them.

Some strong feelings you might experience while you're grieving are:

Loneliness

Numbness

Guilt

Anxiety

Shock

Helplessness

Relief

Freedom

Sadness

If you're grieving, which feelings are you experiencing most strongly right now? Work through them all, one at a time, and really feel where you're holding these emotions in your body. For example, some people hold anxiety in their chest and sadness in their stomach.

Now you've worked out where you're holding these feelings, I'd like you to carry out the breathing exercise above, and let light wash into these areas until they feel relaxed and open.

The aim is not to get rid of your feelings, but to learn to feel calm beside them. These feelings are there for a reason and must run their course. We're looking to grow around them, in order to reach a place of calm and peace.

Psychic Consultation

A lady called Jo visited me after her sister had passed away. She was, in her own words, 'a very busy lady', and always 'on the go'. She found it very hard to sit still, and I could tell by her manner that she was in a stressed state.

Jo told me that soon after her sister had passed away, she'd actually felt calmer and more like herself than ever before. She got on well with her family while they arranged the funeral, and, although she felt sad, she felt more loving and open than she had in a long time.

As time passed, though, she slipped back into bad habits. She still carried the sadness of her sister's death, but now she had a heavy workload and family commitments on top of that. She was overworked and under pressure, and just didn't know how to switch off.

I knew that, while she was in this highly agitated state, connecting with her sister would be difficult. I brought calm into myself and made a connection to the spirits, and Jo's sister came through for a short time. However, I knew we could make contact for longer if Jo could let go of her stress.

I gave Jo details of a local meditation class, and urged her to start taking sessions. Her first thoughts were that this 'wouldn't be for her', but since the classes were free and very close to her home, I persuaded her that she had nothing to lose.

A month later, Jo came back to me a much calmer woman. Meditation had quite literally changed her life. She was able to feel much more relaxed, content and loving, and bring herself back into the calmer state that grief had forced upon her.

We made a strong connection with her sister during our second session, and I could tell Jo really accepted and enjoyed the love she got from the spirit world.

Chapter Ten:

Making Contact: the Seven Steps

to the Spirits

Now that you've learned to calm your mind and get into a meditative state, it's time to try and make contact with the spirits. Some of you will be excited by this. Others, a little nervous. No matter how you feel, I promise you life is about to change in the most wonderful way. I'm now going to talk you through the seven stages of making contact, but please remember that reaching the spirits takes lots of practice. I don't expect any of you to succeed first time. My motto is try, try and try again.

STEP ONE: CHOOSING THE VENUE

First and foremost, I'd like you to think about *where* you'd like to make contact with your loved one. For first-timers, I'd recommend choosing a place that was special to the departed, and where you can clearly picture them enjoying life.

Take your time thinking over where you'd like to make contact, and remember it must be a place where you yourself will feel happy and safe. For example, I wouldn't recommend a park in winter. You should be warm and comfortable.

When the spirits come through, they are vital and in great health.

You don't have to choose a totally private venue, but if you choose somewhere public, make sure people won't approach you or try to talk to you. You must be in a space where you feel totally safe and secure, and are able to let go of your conscious mind.

Often, our own homes make the very best places to contact the spirits. If your loved one lived with you, you might choose their favourite area of the house, or a place you can easily picture them.

I wouldn't recommend choosing a place where your loved one was ill – especially if that illness led to their passing. When the spirits come through, they are vital and in great health. All sickness and old age is gone, and they are in the prime of their life. If you choose an area connected with illness, the spirits may not want to come through.

STEP TWO: RAISING THE VIBRATIONS

The spirit world operates at a higher vibration than we do here on earth. Spirits are made up of light, loose energy that flows freely, whereas down here in the physical realm, things are heavier and more solid.

It's a good idea to raise the vibrations of a space before you try to make contact, and a great way to do this is by playing music or singing. The spirits love to hear our voices, and they love music too.

If you're able to play some uplifting music, or sing a few songs in the space you've chosen to make contact, this will really help lift the vibrations of where you are and get the spirits flowing around you.

STEP THREE: CONNECTING WITH CALM

Remember the 'Connecting with Your Intuition Exercise' in Chapter Four? I asked you to take deep breaths and fill your body with white light.

I'd like you to carry out that exercise now, as the first step to contacting the spirits, remembering everything you've learned about meditation and feeling calm.

Before you start, make sure that you're entirely comfortable. Loosen any tight clothing, remove your shoes and check that, if you're at home, any locks or windows are as you'd like them to be. Relaxing into a meditative state requires a total feeling of safety, so make sure there won't be any sudden noises that will jolt you out of your calm state.

Once your body is feeling soft and calm and relaxed, and your mind is free of everyday concerns and in a dreamlike state, you are almost ready to connect with the spirits.

STEP FOUR: THE OPENING PRAYER OR AFFIRMATION

Before calling upon the spirits, I usually say a short prayer or affirmation to make my intentions clear to the spirit world. The affirmation changes a little, depending on whom I wish to make contact with, but it always has the same sentiment. Here are the sorts of words I use:

> *With love and light, I welcome the spirits today.*
> *I invite the spirits to use my body as a channel to share their messages of love.*

I place a golden band around myself to help me focus on the spirits I would like to talk to. Today, I ask that my departed loved ones come through. I accept love and light from the spirit world, in whatever form it comes.

You are very welcome to write your own prayer or affirmation, as this will have more meaning for you. You can use any words that are special to you, including lines from the poems, prayers or affirmations of others.

Write your prayer or affirmation on a nice, thick piece of paper, or in a special book or diary, and read it out loud or in your head.

STEP FIVE: BUILDING A BRIDGE TO THE SPIRITS

Now that you've calmed down and read your affirmation, it's time to start building a bridge to the spirit world.

The spirits live among us, but on a different plane. We need to build a bridge between our physical world and the light, dream-like place where the spirits live.

From your calm, meditative state of mind, I'd like you to feel the weight of your earthly body. If your feet are on the ground, feel the earth beneath them and how heavily you stand on the earth. Feel how your body pulls down towards the ground, and feel your clothes against your skin. You are in the physical world, and the physical world is heavy and solid.

Once you cross the bridge, you are ready to meet the spirits.

Now I'd like you to feel the lightness and energy of the spirit world above you. Feel the flow of air and how fluid it is. You can't grab hold of it. You can't touch it. You can only feel it with your intuitive sense.

Imagine that your body is now becoming lighter, like the air above you. You are leaving behind the weight of your body, and your intuitive mind is travelling out of the physical realm and up, up to join the spirits.

As you float up out of your body, you will see a beautiful bridge stretched out before you. The bridge is no colour that you recognise, but it sparkles like clear water on a summer's day.

The bridge is shrouded in light white cloud, so you can't see what's on the other side. But you know in your heart that your loved ones are there, waiting for you.

I'd like you to travel now along the bridge. You won't be using your earthly body. Instead, your intuitive mind will float across.

Once you cross the bridge, you are ready to meet the spirits. You may not hear or see anything once you reach the other side, but you should feel in yourself that you have crossed to another place – a place where the spirits are waiting.

STEP SIX: ASKING THE SPIRITS TO COME FORWARDS

Now that your intuitive mind has joined the spirits, it is time to ask them to come forwards.

Ask in a clear, bold voice: 'If there is anyone in spirit here, would you please step forwards?'

You don't have to use your earthly voice, although you can if you feel it gives you more power. However, the intuitive voice in your head will work just fine.

Now you wait. This is probably the hardest part for any beginner, because often you won't get anything at all the first few times you cross the bridge. In the early days, you're likely to experience fleeting glimpses of things, or shadows of voices. Nothing will be clear or certain, and you won't know which spirit you're making contact with.

This is perfectly normal and natural, but it can feel very frustrating – especially if you're very eager to make contact. I have to tell you that the more frustrated you feel, the harder making contact will be. You simply can't try too hard when it comes to the spirits. You have to hold on to things lightly and accept whatever comes.

You may hear music, laughter and singing.

The more you practise, the more sights and sounds from the spirit world will grow clearer. Whole words, faded pictures and old memories will start to float into your mind. As time goes on, these words will become whole sentences and the pictures will become clearer. You may hear music, laughter and singing.

These sights and sounds are the spirits making contact. Your job is to piece together what you are seeing and hearing, and try to understand what the spirits are trying to tell you. Because they are communicating from another plane, at a higher vibration and using completely different energy than we do here on earth, interpreting their messages is something that takes time and skill. But I promise you, the more you practise, the better you will get.

The most important thing is how you feel. If you feel loving energy, then you can be assured that the spirits are around you.

As soon as you get that strong feeling of love, even if you haven't seen or heard anything from the spirits, then you must ask:

'What is your name?'

Then listen for the answer. You may be shown a memory or a

picture, or hear a word. From these things, you must determine who is coming through for you.

You should then ask:

'How did you die?'

This question will also help you piece together who the spirit is. It won't always be the person you expect, but it will always be somebody who loves you.

Without fail, my grandfather comes through for me first. He then brings through the spirits of others. You may find that an older spirit – one who has been in the spirit realm for a long time – will help you find newer spirits. In the spirit world, the age when someone died doesn't matter. It is their spiritual age, and their time in spirit, that is important.

I always say that the spirit world is a bit like a bus stop. You never quite know who you're going to encounter. In some ways, whichever spirit shouts the loudest is the one you'll hear. So if a loved one has a particular message for you, you may hear them louder than another loved one whom you were very close to.

STEP SEVEN: TRY, TRY AND TRY AGAIN

For most beginners, the first few attempts to make contact are tricky. You may see and hear a few things, but nothing you can really grab hold of, and nothing that tells you for certain which spirit is coming through.

I would say that if you receive any messages at all from the spirits during your first three attempts, you are doing very well indeed. Calming down, tuning in and building a bridge between here and the spirit world takes a lot of practice, and many, many attempts before you start hearing clear messages and knowing for certain which spirits you're talking to.

Just like anything in life, the more you try, the better you'll get. Be patient and keep going. I promise you'll get there.

Psychic Consultation

When I first started channelling the spirits for others, I didn't always manage to make contact with anyone other than my grandfather. Of course, I never charged for these early sessions, but I always used to wonder how on earth people worked as mediums for a living, since the path to the spirits felt so shaky and uncertain in those early days.

However, the more I practised channelling for others, the clearer the messages from the spirits became. I remember one magical session where I made contact for three different people in a row, and shared with them how their loved ones had died, and messages of love. From that day on, I made contact for other people every time I tried.

I never dreamed, when I first started out, that I'd be able to read so clearly every time, but I'm here to tell you that practice makes perfect. If I can do it, so can you!

Chapter Eleven:

Hearing the Spirits

The spirits talk through our intuition, and we must remember that the intuitive mind is not a logical place. It doesn't do things in order, or work with time very well. Therefore, it's important to learn *how* your intuition may try to share messages from the spirits.

Sometimes the spirits will tell you something loud and clear. On other occasions, your intuition will see symbols or flashes of colour, and from these you'll have to work out what the spirits are sharing. I'd like now to look at some of the things you might see and hear while you're connected with the spirit world, and share how to interpret messages that aren't straightforward or obvious.

HOW THE DEPARTED SPEAK THROUGH SYMBOLS

The intuitive, psychic mind is a great lover of symbols. When it connects with the spirits, it will often interpret what they are saying by flashing up a symbolic object.

What do I mean by 'symbol'? Well, there are certain things that we as human beings understand to have great meaning and importance. We don't necessarily know why we place such meaning and importance on them, but we do.

Our intuition has a great understanding of symbols.

For example, rings and circles have a great deal of significance to human beings. We put wedding rings on our fingers to symbolise union, and from ancient times we have used round clearings and tables for important meetings.

Another important symbol for us humans is water. We use water to baptise babies in religious ceremonies, and pools of water decorate our gardens and parks. Water is the symbol of birth and life.

Our intuition has a great understanding of symbols. Because our intuition represents our psychic side and our soul, it knows what symbols mean and *feels* something when they appear. Our logical mind, on the other hand, doesn't really understand them. Since symbols are all to do with feelings and our subconscious, our logical side doesn't see their importance at all.

I'm going to give you a strange example of symbols now. Star Wars! I'm guessing you've watched the Star Wars films – who hasn't? These films are absolutely packed with symbols. The white robed Jedi and the black caped Darth Vader. The twin boy and girl, Luke and Leia, and the shrivelled wise man, Yoda. Lightsabers (swords) and the princess held prisoner. All of these things link to very potent ancient symbols that speak clearly to our intuition.

There's a reason why the first Star Wars films are so popular, even forty years after they were first made. Symbols! The symbols in these films have very strong links with our intuitive mind.

I'm going to give you a brief list of important symbols, and a loose explanation of their meanings. However, don't focus too heavily on the meanings I give. Focus on what your feelings tell you when you think of these symbols, and you'll understand what they mean.

Psychic Symbols

Water – life, birth and rebirth
Fire – passion, healing and strength
Rings – bonding and friendship
Houses and rooms – our bodies and their different parts
Books – learning and knowledge
Vehicles – change and escape
Money and jewellery – security and safety
Wings and feathers – freedom and the afterlife
An old man or woman – wisdom

When you connect with the spirits, strange words and pictures may float into your mind. If any of these are symbols, pay close attention because these are powerful messages from the spirits. Work with your feelings to try to understand what these symbols mean, and what the spirits are trying to tell you.

Let me give you an example. Some time ago, I was reading for a lady who wanted to connect with her departed aunt. The two women had been close, and this lady, who was called Karen, had nursed her aunt through a long illness. It had been a sad and painful time.

We connected with the spirit world, and Karen's aunt came forwards. Although she looked happy and healthy, as spirits always do, I had an image of her sitting in a very small dark attic room. The attic room was so small that when this lady reached up to the ceiling, she could put her palms flat against it.

> *There are all sorts of ways in which the spirits use symbols to tell us what they mean.*

I had an image of Karen's aunt pushing hard against the ceiling until it lifted, and white light flooding in. The walls of the room fell away, and white light surrounded her. She smiled, waved and then disappeared.

I explained my vision to Karen and told her how houses and rooms symbolise our bodies. Since Karen's aunt was in the attic, I reasoned she was trying to tell us something about her mind. Attics and roofs generally symbolise the head and face, since they're at the top of the house.

I thought about the small, dark room and asked Karen if her aunt had some sort of illness that made her less able to think clearly. I had a real sense of darkness closing in around this lady's mind and thought processes.

Karen said yes – her aunt had suffered dementia before she passed. She'd been a very intelligent, funny lady before the illness, and the loss of her memory and ability to think straight had caused her a great deal of confusion and pain.

I was able to tell Karen that her aunt was now completely free of this suffering. All pain ends when we are in spirit, of course, but the fact Karen's aunt had wanted to share this particular image told me she was trying to reassure Karen that she was happy now, and free of her illness.

There are all sorts of ways in which the spirits use symbols to tell us what they mean. They may whisper words or flash up images. They may even draw your attention to something nearby, in the material world, and urge you to focus on it.

I've had my attention drawn to fountains, feathers and coins before. The spirits certainly do like their symbols!

COLOURFUL SPIRITS

Our intuition loves colours – the brighter the better. When we connect to the spirit world, especially during the early days, we may see nothing more than flashes of colour. This can be dispiriting, since most of us hope to see a walking, talking image of our loved one. But colours can tell you more than you think.

The intuition uses colours to share messages with us, and colours have a very strong link with feelings and psychic energy.

When we see colours during our psychic connections, they can be the beginnings of messages from our loved ones. Once you understand what the colours may be saying, you will be closer to hearing your loved one in spirit.

I will now share with you what certain colours have meant for me, when they've cropped up during a psychic connection. However, remember to listen to your own feelings. What do they tell you when you see a certain colour?

White

The most common colour people see, when they connect to the spirit world, is white. A lovely, pure white light. White is a very reassuring colour. It cheers us up and chases away fear and concern. When we see white in the spirit world, we are being told that everything is okay. No one is in pain here or afraid. This is a calm, peaceful and loving place.

Orange

Orange is another extremely common colour to see when you connect to the spirits. You may see it as hazy lines, a ball of light or a bright flash. Although orange will have its own meanings to you, I usually find that it's linked to wisdom, knowledge and advice. It often appears when the spirits are trying to share something with you from their world, that is not obvious in yours.

For example, a fellow psychic shared with me a connection she made while she was buying a new car. She freely admitted she'd been obsessing over getting her new car, and could think of little else. When she connected with the spirit of her departed mother, she saw a strong flash of orange and heard the words 'the car doesn't matter!' This was her dear old mum trying to remind her what was *really* important in life. For the spirits, all material things seem a little silly. And of course, when all is said and done they're right, aren't they? After all, you can't take it with you!

Red

Red is a very passionate and bright colour, and I often find it's connected with loving thoughts and feelings. When red appears during a connection, it's usually because a spirit is trying very hard to share love from the afterlife. For most of us, it's lovely to get red during a psychic connection. However, do listen to your feelings, as for some red can feel like a warning sign. If you feel uneasy when you see red, this may be a sign that you should be cautious in some area of your life.

Blue

I find that blue doesn't come up all that often during a psychic connection, but when it does it points to health and healing. The spirits are trying to send healing energy to you down here on earth, or urging you to slow down and seek medical advice. If there is something health-wise that's been niggling you, the spirits are urging you to pay attention.

Green

Green is the colour of nature, and often crops up when the spirits are trying to tell us about living in harmony with others. It's a colour of friendship, so it also points towards renewing old friendships or working on existing ones. When green appears during a connection, I find it's usually because the spirits are urging us to put our lives in balance, and create harmony with others. If we're having a petty squabble about something, it's time to let it go.

I saw a flash of green during a consultation with a client who was still furious with her brother over her father's funeral arrangements. It had been many months since the funeral, but this lady was angry that her brother hadn't contributed to the finances or arrangements.

I explained that when I see green, it usually means the spirits want us to let things go and rebuild relationships. I asked if there was someone she'd fallen out with, and she explained about her anger towards her brother. She admitted that she'd been carrying the anger around far too long, and that her departed father would want her to let it go.

The above is a very basic explanation of colours during your psychic visions, but as I mentioned before, do please listen to your own feelings first and foremost. The most important thing to remember is that, even if you don't believe you've seen or heard much during a connection, a flash of colour can be a powerful message from the spirits. Don't discount colours if you see them. Feel what they want you to feel.

ASKING THE SPIRITS FOR CLARITY

The spirits try to talk to us in all sorts of strange and creative ways, and one of the most useful lessons to learn is that you can ask the spirits for more clarity. If you see colours, symbols or images, but don't understand what they mean, it's perfectly okay to ask the spirits to make things clearer.

> *Your job is simply to ask the spirits to tell you more, keep connecting whenever you can and wait patiently.*

They may not always respond straight away. Most commonly, they'll send you more answers in your dreams, or clearer images the next time you connect.

When it comes to the spirits, you have to be patient. The more you connect, the more messages you'll receive and the clearer the previous messages will become. Slowly but surely, you will build up a picture of what your loved ones want to share, but it may take time. Your job is simply to ask the spirits to tell you more, keep connecting whenever you can and wait patiently.

The spirits don't have a great sense of time. For them, they have all the time in the world. Sometimes they forget that down here on earth, time moves along at a fast pace. Getting frustrated or trying to force the spirits to talk will only end in tears. Be patient and all good things will come.

Chapter Twelve:

Using Psychic Cards

I love using cards to help me hear messages from the spirits. They're nothing more than a prop, of course, and you certainly don't *need* them to get in touch. But if you're looking for answers to specific questions, then psychic cards can be a great help.

PSYCHIC READERS AND MEDIUMS

Before we go any further, I'd better explain the difference between mediums and psychic readers.

When you connect with the spirits, you're acting as a medium. This means you're a channel or medium between this world and the next. You use your intuition as part of this process, and your psychic energy senses when the spirits are close and interprets their messages.

A psychic reader, on the other hand, is simply someone who uses their intuitive powers to answer questions – either about their own life or yours. They often use props like cards in their psychic readings.

A medium will always have psychic abilities, but a psychic is not necessarily a medium.

When you use props, like cards, you use the tools of psychic readers to contact the spirits. In the process, sometimes you will find out things about your life that the spirits haven't told you.

Using psychic tools means that, sometimes, your own intuitive inner wisdom will step in when the spirits don't have the answers.

WHAT ARE PSYCHIC CARDS?

Psychic cards are large, colourful playing cards with big, bold illustrations on them. There are literally thousands of different types, and psychics use the pictures and symbols on them to interpret life events. When we use them with the spirits, we allow our departed loved ones to help us choose cards from the deck and share messages through their pictures.

My favourite psychic cards, especially for beginners, are traditional tarot cards, angel cards and the psychic tarot.

Traditional Tarot Cards

Even if you've never seen a deck of tarot cards in real life, you've probably seen the tarot in films or read about them in books. The traditional tarot focuses on ancient symbols and charts the different stages of our journey through life.

The full deck of tarot has 'suits', similar to normal playing cards, and is made up of two groups known as the major and minor arcanas. The major arcana is probably the part of the deck you're most familiar with, as it includes cards such as 'the lovers' and 'death'.

> *I'd recommend forgetting about the traditional explanations of tarot cards, and simply asking your heart what it feels when it looks at the pictures.*

In a traditional tarot deck there's a card for every different eventuality in life. However, the cards hardly ever give definite answers. They're always open to interpretation.

Just to make things even more complicated, there are many different versions of the traditional tarot deck, each with different pictures and sometimes different card names. For beginners, I'd recommend the classic Rider Waite tarot. This is the tarot that will look the most familiar to you.

Tarot cards are good for major life questions. For example, if you're considering moving home after a bereavement or want to try to understand a loss, the tarot can help point you in the right direction.

When it comes to talking to the spirits, I believe the traditional symbols on the tarot help us tune in to the ancient wisdom and power that links us to the afterlife.

I'd recommend forgetting about the traditional explanations of tarot cards, simply asking your heart what it feels when it looks at the pictures instead. You'll find the pictures really speak to you, and you'll see and hear all sorts of things. Sometimes, things in the cards will appear to move around to help you understand their meaning.

To use tarot cards, you need to know a few basic spreads. I'll share two very simple ones with you in a moment.

Angel Cards

Angel cards can be a good way to link with the spirits, as they're all about connecting with the angels or higher beings – which to me is the same as the spirit world.

In some ways, they stunt the intuition a little, as they usually have a lot of words on each card. However, it can be tremendously comforting to use angel cards when you have lost someone, as they give you a sense that loving, higher beings are watching over you.

You don't need to read the instruction manual that comes with the cards – simply let the pictures guide your intuition.

Just like the tarot, there are many different kinds of angel cards. Some are more religious than others, and generally I like the ones that are more spiritual and less church orientated.

The Angel Tarot, by Doreen Virtue, is a good starting place for beginners. This set has beautiful, detailed pictures and can really give you a sense of loving spirits all around.

You don't have to be religious at all to use angel cards. You just have to be open to the messages they share.

The wonderful thing about angel cards is that you don't need to use spreads, as such. You simply hold them to your heart, ask the question you desire and ask your loved one to help you. Shuffle the cards and ask your loved one to guide you to the card or cards that will give you the answer.

You don't need to read the instruction manual that comes with the cards – simply let the pictures guide your intuition.

The Psychic Tarot by John Holland

These are my favourite of all psychic cards, and perfect for beginners. This particular psychic tarot set is filled with beautiful, detailed pictures that really spark the imagination. They're extremely colourful, too, which is great for bringing out your intuitive self.

Just like any psychic cards, you don't need to read the instructions when you use the psychic tarot – just let the pictures speak to you. Unlike angel cards, the psychic tarot only has one word on each card to help guide you. I prefer this to the rather wordy angel cards, as language can trip up your intuitive self.

Like traditional tarot cards, you can use the psychic tarot in a spread. Or simply fan them out and pick the cards that speak to you. It's entirely up to you.

SPREADS

Traditionally, psychic cards are placed in a certain formation, depending on the questions you're looking to answer. Cards mean different things in different positions.

Spreads can be very complicated, but I like to keep things simple. So here are two very easy spreads that you can use to ask questions of your loved ones in spirit.

Past, Present and Future

For this spread, shuffle the cards until a warm, calm feeling washes over you. Then choose, at random, three cards from the pack. Choose whichever cards seem to 'pull' you towards them. Lay them face down in a line. The first card represents the past. The middle represents the present, and the last card on the right-hand side represents the future.

Once you've laid out your three cards, turn the 'past' card over. Allow yourself as long as you need to absorb the messages the spirits are trying to share. Remember that this card is about your past. The spirits are sharing how they interpret your recent past, helping you see things that you may not have noticed.

The spirits only want what's best for you, and will never share messages that aren't in your best interests.

Now turn over the 'present' card. This card represents your current situation, and the spirits will be trying to tell you where you *really* are. Things may be better than you had realised, or more challenging.

Once you've absorbed the messages on this card, turn over the 'future' card. This should help you answer your question, and will show you where you're going. If you like the look of where you're going, then great. If not, the spirits are trying to warn you about something and steer you away from the path you're on.

Don't be afraid – all mistakes can be corrected. The spirits only want what's best for you, and will never share messages that aren't in your best interests.

This spread is great for assessing life situations and asking big questions.

The One Card

You may have guessed by the title of this spread that it's, well – just one card! And it's as simple as that. Shuffle the cards until you feel warm and relaxed. Then choose a card from the deck – this can be any card that seems to leap out at you, from any part of the deck. Lay out this card face down. Then turn it over and take in what the card has to say.

This spread is good for simple questions and quick answers. I love using it when I have a very straightforward question to ask. When life is a little more complicated, I use the past, present and future spread.

TUNING IN TO THE SPIRITS WITH CARDS

Before you tune in, you should get familiar with your cards and make sure your energy is imparted to them – especially if they're new.

With a brand-new pack of cards, I'd suggest giving yourself at least half an hour to look through them before you do a reading. The act of moving the cards between your hands will help impart your energy to them, and the more familiar you become with the pictures, the easier it will be to receive psychic messages.

You'll know your loved one is nearby when you feel a deep sense of calm spread over your whole body.

The way you tune in to the spirits when you're using psychic cards is similar to how you'd usually do it. Relax, take some time to steady your breathing and then let white light travel up and down your body. Feel loving energy pass through you, and allow your body to become warm and relaxed.

Remember, with psychic cards you're asking the spirits to help you with a specific question. So once you're filled with light, intuitive energy, take your cards and shuffle them, thinking the whole time about the question you'd like to ask.

Once you've shuffled and asked your question, focus on your loved one and bring their energy to you. You'll know your loved one is nearby when you feel a deep sense of calm spread over your whole body.

Only ask one question at a time, and be really specific about what you'd like to know. Talking to the spirits is a bit like choosing a holiday. You have to have a clear idea of your destination, otherwise you'll never get anywhere.

Psychic Consultation

I used the psychic tarot for a lady who'd lost her husband some years ago. She was still living in the family home, and didn't want to leave for fear of losing precious memories of her old life. However, looking after the home on her own was becoming a burden.

She wanted to ask her husband if it was the right time to move house.

We sat quietly and I asked my client to shuffle the cards and impart her energy to them. Then I took the cards and laid out a simple past, present, future spread.

In this lady's past sat the 'achievements' card, which suggested her husband was trying to remind her how proud the two of them had been to buy their own home.

The present card was the 'patience' card, and the future card was the 'spiritual union' card.

I explained to the lady that her husband was advising her to take her time, and that some sort of divine happening would come soon to help make her decision.

A few months later, the lady returned to me with some wonderful news. She'd been reunited with a childhood friend, and the two had become very close – so close that she was considering moving him into her home.

Now she had the option of running her home with two people in it again. She was glad she'd waited before selling her home, as in her heart she didn't really want to live by herself. Because she still had the old family home, there was plenty of space for someone else to move in.

This reading proved to me once again what I've always known about the spirits. They're never jealous or selfish and always have our best interests at heart. I can't imagine many husbands in the earthly realm being happy about their wives living with a new man!

HOW TO ASK THE RIGHT QUESTIONS

The spirits like clear, simple questions, so take some time to get your question right before you make contact. Your question doesn't have to be the 'yes/no' type – far from it. But make sure you have a clear understanding of exactly what you want to know. You can't be wishy-washy when asking the spirits questions. You need to be loud and clear.

Once you've asked your question, you'll feel the answers in the cards, but also in your head. The cards will boost your intuition, giving you more images and words to help hear what the spirits are saying.

Although I like using psychic cards, I would urge you to remember that they are nothing more than a prop. Used in the right way, they can be wonderful, but don't grow to rely on them too heavily. You can easily hear the spirits without them.

Chapter Thirteen:

Connecting with Psychic Circles

Connecting with a departed loved one on your own is a very beautiful and personal experience. However, some of us enjoy having this experience in a group setting too, and benefiting from the mutual support of others when the connection is over. Of course, you don't have to choose one way or another. You can connect by yourself when you feel like it, or with groups when you'd like companionship and support.

This chapter is all about making connections with the spirits in a group setting, and finding like-minded people to connect to the spirit world with you.

I call a group connection a 'psychic circle', and it really can be a wonderful way of discovering love and support during a difficult time.

WHY THE SPIRITS LIKE GATHERINGS

Human beings are social creatures, and most of us like being around others. The spirits are no different. When big groups of people come together in life, especially if that group love and care about each other, the spirits will tend to gather around too.

The spirits are attracted to energy, and a large group of people all enjoying life together, or crying together over the loss of a loved one, creates a large body of energy that draws the spirits closer.

The spirits particularly like groups of people singing or chanting in unison, which goes some way to explaining why most religions have shared songs and prayers that are spoken out loud.

When there is a large group gathered to connect with the afterlife, at least one spirit will almost always come through. The power of the group is so strong that it's hard for the spirits to stay away. In fact, it's much easier to connect with the spirit world when you're in company. The downside is, it's harder to bring forward any specific spirits. Many different spirits will be swirling around during a group gathering. It's usually simply a question of hearing who is shouting the loudest.

Sometimes people leave a psychic circle disappointed that they didn't make a connection with their loved one. However, the positive side is that at least one person in the group almost always makes a connection.

The key to a psychic circle is to meet regularly.

When you connect to the spirits with a group of people, it's like supercharging the pathway to the spirit world. Because you're throwing the door open so wide, lots of spirits come through. When you're alone, the connection is much looser and weaker, but you're more likely to bring through the spirit of your departed loved one.

You may not meet your departed loved one when you take part in a group connection, or 'psychic circle', but what you will gain is a whole host of love and support. Others who have lost loved ones and want to connect with them will not only understand your loss, they will also share your belief in the afterlife and the spirits. This can provide great comfort and companionship during a difficult and often lonely time.

The key to a psychic circle is to meet regularly. On some occasions your loved one will come through, but on others they won't. In the meantime, you can offer love and support to your friends, and rejoice when your energy helps bring through the spirits of loved ones for others.

SÉANCES

Psychic circles take on many forms, and one of those is the 'séance'. A séance refers to a group of people, led by a medium, who are gathered together to contact the spirit world.

Séances have something of a bad reputation, thanks to con artists using them to make a quick profit out of grieving people. However, there are many good séances held all around the country on a regular basis, hosted by genuine mediums whose only interest is in helping others.

If you visit a séance, you should expect to pay between £5 and £10 for entry, which covers the cost of the venue and the medium's transport costs and time.

Unlike TV portrayals of séances as dark and spooky gatherings, most séances are now held in bright, modern buildings, and sometimes during the daytime. Guests are made to feel warm and comfortable, and often there is a social gathering before or after the séance, where drinks and food are served.

A séance is hosted by a professional medium, who will stand in front of the group and begin channelling the spirits.

Some séances, especially those held in spiritualist churches, will begin with singing. Others simply begin when the medium arrives.

The medium will generally talk about each spirit they see, and ask if anyone in the group feels a connection with this spirit. They will then share messages from the spirit world.

Regular séances can be a nice way to meet like-minded people, but you certainly don't need to attend a paid-for séance to make a group connection with the spirit world. Let's talk now about how you can make your own psychic circle.

BUILDING A PSYCHIC CIRCLE

A psychic circle is really a very simple thing. All you need is a group of people – I'd say at least five is best, but I think three can work as a minimum. The more people taking part, the better. You also need a calm and relaxing venue – somewhere comfortable and peaceful. This can be someone's living room, or a hired hall. In warm weather, you can take your psychic circle outside and connect with the spirits in the garden under the sun or the moon. It's a very beautiful thing to connect with your loved ones when nature is all around.

You need someone to lead the circle, but that person can change at each gathering. You don't have to have a single leader as such, but every time you meet, someone should take responsibility for opening and closing the connection.

It might be a good idea to hire a professional medium for your first psychic circle, as he or she can help smooth any nerves and speed up the connection.

I'd recommend that before you try to connect with the spirits, your group take part in some social activity together.

Prepare a seating area for the group where, ideally, everyone can sit around in a circle. If this isn't possible, it's fine to sit in a semicircle or even in rows, but everyone should be able to see whoever is leading the session.

I prefer a circular arrangement, because I think it creates a ring of energy that brings the spirits closer. It also means that, if you choose, you can all hold hands. You don't have to hold hands, of course, but I think it gives the group a nice bond and a more powerful energy.

I'd recommend that before you try to connect with the spirits, your group take part in some social activity together. Perhaps a meal, or just a cup of tea and a chat. The idea is to make sure you're all connecting with one another, and feeling at ease in each other's company before you begin.

When your group are feeling relaxed and talkative, sit them in your designated area. You can dim the lights if you wish. However, some people feel a little frightened by the idea of 'bad spirits' when the lights are low, so it's perfectly acceptable to connect in brightness.

Whoever is leading the gathering should close their eyes and take some time to feel calm. This is where a professional medium comes in handy, as they can feel calm within minutes.

If you or another group member is leading the connection, tell the group how long it usually takes you to feel calm and connected, so they can anticipate how long they will have to wait.

The job of the leader is to hear each spirit one at a time, and try to place them with their living friend or relative.

Once the leader is calm, it is time to ask the spirits to come forwards. All that is needed is for the leader to say:

'Is there anyone out there?'

Unlike when you connect alone, everything must be said out loud.

If you yourself are making the connection, you will be surprised at the rush of chatter and images that come forwards during a group gathering. It's a very different experience to connecting alone. When we make a personal connection with our loved one, we often struggle to hear words and only see flashes of images. However, in a group it's a different story! So many spirits will be clambering to come forwards. The job of the leader is to hear each spirit one at a time, and try to place them with their living friend or relative.

I must say, it's not an easy task leading a psychic circle, and the rush of sounds and images can be very confusing at first. But if your group is understanding, you will over time get better and better at hearing the individual messages and understanding who is coming through, and for whom.

FINDING LIKE-MINDED PEOPLE

The best way to find other people who are interested in creating a psychic circle is to talk to your friends. Start with anyone you know who already has an interest in spirits and mediumship, and ask if they know anyone else who may be interested in forming a circle. Talking with people you know is the very best way to build your psychic circle, and you'll be surprised at how quickly friends and friends of friends will come forwards to join you.

You can also find like-minded people at spiritualist churches and other organisations that deal in spirit connections.

If you're really struggling, ask the spirits to bring people forwards. I promise that if you're committed to forming a psychic circle, you will create one quickly and easily.

Psychic Consultation

A few years ago, I connected for a lady who had lost her husband. The lady had not long retired, and most of her social life had revolved around activities for couples with her husband. Now he had passed, she was finding it difficult to socialise with her old group as a 'lonely widow', as all her friends were still in couples and took part in activities like group tennis which were very much designed for two.

Not only this, but her old friends weren't at all open-minded about the more spiritual side of life, and didn't believe in life after death. She knew they didn't take her seriously when she spoke about her husband's spirit, and that some thought she was 'going batty' after the loss.

I advised this lady, whose name was Janet, to visit a local spiritualist church, where she could meet other people who were interested in making spiritual connections. These people would also, in the main, have lost someone close, so she was likely to meet others in the same life position as herself.

We found a spiritual church near where Janet lived, and I sent her off to a séance that very night.

The next time we met, Janet was glowing. She'd met all sorts of interesting and open-minded people at the séance, and had a good, long chat with a fellow widow who lived only a few streets away. The two ladies had met several times since for coffee, and were well on the way to becoming good friends.

Janet still came to me to make a personal connection with her husband's spirit, as she had yet to connect with him at a séance. But for her, that wasn't the point of attending spiritual gatherings. She liked group connections because they were a great place to talk about her husband's spirit, and meet others who shared her beliefs.

SPIRITUAL CHURCHES AND GROUPS

You may find that once you start meeting others who are interested in connecting with the spirits, you discover a whole new group of friends. You may also discover new talents and interests.

When you are open to psychic energy, you will learn many new things about the powers we human beings have within us. You may find that you become interested in more than just mediumship, and you might start exploring new ways to use your psychic powers.

Spiritual churches are great places to meet others who are interested in psychic powers and spiritual connections, and they often hold regular séances and gatherings where you can socialise and meet new people. Most towns and cities have a spiritualist church. Check www.thespiritualist.org/ for details of spiritualist groups near you.

Chapter Fourteen:

Bad Spirits

Thanks to horror films and scary TV shows, many of us worry about bad spirits. We fear that the afterlife, at least in part, may be a bleak, evil place where spirits go when they haven't found peace. Ghost stories tell us that some spirits haunt houses and graveyards in an attempt to hurt the living.

I'm here to tell you that nothing in the afterlife can harm you and there is no such thing as a bad spirit. However, it's worth working through some of the myths and rumours about ghosts so you can put your mind at rest, and understand why you may feel uneasy in so-called haunted buildings.

I'll also share with you a cleansing exercise for those of you who can't shake your fears of bad spirits, and a protection exercise to stop any unwanted spirits coming through. By unwanted, I don't mean bad. But as your psychic powers grow, there may be times when you'd like to close the door to all the many spirits wanting to talk to you.

THINGS THAT GO BUMP IN THE NIGHT

I believe that most stories of bad spirits are just that – stories. Bad spirits are just our own fears, *or* our own desire to see something spooky. How many of us, as teenagers, used a Ouija board or visited a graveyard on Halloween to try and see something scary? And of course, it's much more fun when you believe you really did see something scary, isn't it?

Looking for bad spirits can be a fun game, but the truth is there are no bad spirits. The afterlife is a happy, peaceful place where all human concerns and petty squabbles disappear.

Even people who were unhappy in life feel contented and at peace in the afterlife. It is a place where all pain and suffering disappears, and we are truly our best selves.

I believe one of the reasons we worry about bad spirits is because the spirits like to show themselves by making things move. This can be frightening if we don't understand the afterlife. It can make us feel as though there are evil ghosts at large, trying to harm us.

> *When you're truly connected with the spirit world, you'll experience such a strong feeling of love and peace that nothing will frighten you.*

I've had many experiences of books falling from bookcases, televisions spontaneously turning on and white feathers appearing in the strangest places.

These experiences are simply the spirits making themselves known in the only way they know how. They don't mean to be frightening or malicious. All they want to do is show you that they're there.

When you're truly connected with the spirit world, you'll experience such a strong feeling of love and peace that nothing will frighten you. You won't worry about things moving. You'll just feel what the spirits want you to feel – their presence.

HAUNTED HOUSES

I'm sure many of you have walked into a place and felt that something wasn't quite right. You might have felt cold, even though the temperature was warm, or just had a general feeling of unease.

You've also, I'm sure, heard stories about haunted houses, castles or ruins. Plenty of famous buildings are said to be haunted, and there are many reports of people seeing or feeling things in these supposedly haunted places.

I personally feel that when you have a strange or uneasy feeling in a place, this is your intuition talking – but not necessarily about the spirits.

Your intuition can tell you all sorts of things about a place that your logical mind might take many months to figure out. Your intuition looks after you. If there is something in a place that is bad for your health – perhaps damp that will affect your lungs, or a lack of sunlight that will put you in a gloomy mood – your intuition will feel it before your mind does.

> *If you're not in tune with your intuition, it's easy to mistake its warning signs for ghostly activity.*

Your intuition doesn't want you to be anywhere that may be bad for you. I believe that some of the most 'haunted' places are simply places that affect most people's health in a negative way. They're usually old and damp and falling apart. Your intuition doesn't want you to be in a place where the ceiling might collapse, or your breathing might suffer. So it sends out all sorts of warning signs asking you to leave.

You'll notice that there are rarely any reports of living humans being hurt or killed in so-called 'haunted' places. People talk of ghostly visions or voices, or strange smells, but nothing more.

This is because stories of evil ghosts and malicious hauntings stem from people's imaginations, often inspired by warning signs from their intuitions. If you're not in tune with your intuition, it's easy to mistake its warning signs for ghostly activity.

I, like many of us, love the 'haunted house' programmes on television, in which the presenters visit so-called 'haunted' places. They're great for entertainment, but please remember, they're not real!

PREVENTING BAD EXPERIENCES

I believe that negative experiences with the spirit world are caused by two things: inexperience and fear.

When people are inexperienced and don't truly understand the spirit world, they carry all sorts of frightening pictures and images of nasty ghosts and ghouls in their minds.

If you try to make contact with the afterlife without truly understanding what it is, or putting yourself in the right calm, peaceful frame of mind, you most likely won't make contact at all. Instead, you will use your imagination to project what you want or *expect* to see.

Since we're all brought up with ghost stories and Halloween, many people's expectation of the spirit world is of distressed or angry ghosts who are not at peace. Instead of understanding that the afterlife is a place where we all go when we pass over, the inexperienced among us believe that only discontent people stay with us in spirit.

It's not helpful to fear bad spirits when you're trying to connect.

This is absolutely not the case. The truth is the exact opposite.

Spirits connect with us to share love, and for no other reason. They don't care about petty quarrels or discontentment from their time on earth. All they want to do is show how much they love you.

The other factor that creates bad experiences is fear. When you feel frightened, you block all the loving, peaceful and calm feelings that should be filling you up when you try to make contact.

We fear all sorts of things when it comes to connecting with the spirits, and I've covered much of how to overcome these fears in earlier chapters. However, I'd like to take a moment to discuss our fears of bad spirits, in particular.

If you have frightening and fearful pictures of bad spirits in your mind, it's going to be difficult to make contact with the afterlife. It's not helpful to fear bad spirits when you're trying to connect.

I'd like to share now a cleansing exercise that will help you banish bad images and clear your mind.

Cleansing Your Mind Exercise

This is a useful exercise for whenever you're having bad or unwelcome thoughts – particularly about ghosts and bad spirits.

First, I'd like you to get hold of some cedar wood, leaves or oil. Cedar is a cleansing wood, and full of age and wisdom.

Next, I'd like you to go to a place where you feel safe and comfortable. My favourite place is sitting on my bed, but you can choose anywhere at all. It's great to be outdoors for this exercise, as this means you can burn the cedar a little so that it smokes. The smoke will help with the cleansing. However, this exercise works well even if you don't light the cedar. If you're using cedar oil, you can heat this indoors in a special aromatic oil burner.

1. Hold the smoking or unlit cedar in both hands, and face east. Say, either out loud or in your head, 'I call upon the energy of the rising sun and new beginnings to chase away bad thoughts and feelings.'

2. Face south and say or think, 'I call upon the heat of the sun to fire up new positive feelings and help me think well of the spirits.'

3. Face west and say or think, 'I call upon the fading sun to heal me of bad thoughts and feelings.'

4. Face north and say or think, 'I call upon the wisdom of the night to help me understand what is true, and that what is true is always love.'

5. Hold the cedar close to you, or inhale its smoke or fragrance deeply, and allow all bad thoughts to drift away.

If you still feel any fear at all when you make contact with the spirits, then I would urge you to go back to earlier chapters and work on your feelings of calmness and peace. You may need to practise meditation more, and just generally ground yourself better before getting in touch.

Psychic Consultation

A young lady came to see me after the loss of her mother. The lady, who was called Janice, wanted very badly to make contact, but was afraid of 'opening the door', and wanted reassurance that if we connected with the spirit world, she wouldn't be haunted by bad spirits. She was also worried that her mother's spirit might not be at peace, since she'd died suddenly in a car accident.

I told Janice that the afterlife is a place of love and happiness, and the only reason spirits come through is to share feelings of love. I also explained that the afterlife is a place of deep contentment, and that her mother would certainly be happy there.

However, I sensed Janice was still holding on to frightening images of a ghostly afterlife, so I suggested we do a cleansing ceremony with cedar. I heated a little cedar oil and carried out a short ceremony to help Janice rid herself of the scary images in her head.

After this ceremony, Janice was able to let go of her ghostly images somewhat (although not entirely), and we made contact with her mother.

Her mother was a beautiful lady, just like Janice, and full of loving energy for her daughter.

After we made the connection, Janice told me that, after feeling love from her mother, she understood what I meant about the afterlife being a kind place. She said she couldn't believe she'd ever felt afraid about getting in touch.

PROTECTION FROM THE SPIRITS

As I say, I believe that all reports of 'bad' spirits are fairy tales. However, there may be times – especially as you grow more experienced – when you'd like to be left in peace by the spirits. Sometimes, the spirits come to me when I haven't asked to make contact, and I can't welcome them all the time. So I'd like to share with you my knowledge of how to turn away spirits, and also how to protect yourself from any persistent spirits who keep wanting to come through when you'd rather they didn't.

By and large, unless you're already very much in tune with your psychic powers, you won't have to worry about too many spirits coming through in the early days. Your biggest problem will probably be making contact in the first place! But as you grow stronger and make contact more often, you will need to strengthen your control of the connection. So I'd like to share now some ways of doing that.

TURNING AWAY THE SPIRITS

As you grow more aware of your intuition, you may find spirits making contact with you at all times of the day and night – even when you're not consciously trying to tune in. Sometimes the spirits will come into your dreams, and while they will always bring with them feelings of love and peace, sometimes you simply may not wish to see them.

It's very, very simple to turn spirits away. Just ask them to leave. The spirits won't be offended or upset. They understand that for some people, it's just not the right time to see them. Ask a spirit to leave and he or she will. Straight away. It's as simple as that.

THE GOLDEN BAND OF PROTECTION

The more experienced you become, the more you'll encounter spirits whom you've never met in the earthly world. This is exciting, as it means your powers of intuition are becoming very strong indeed, and you'll soon be able to channel spirits for other people, as professional mediums do.

However, it's important that once you get to this level of experience, you're able to keep strong control of your connection with the spirit world.

Before I make contact for other people, I carry out an exercise called the 'Golden Band of Protection'.

This exercise helps me focus on connecting with only the spirits I wish to speak to.

1. After you've calmed yourself down and pictured white light rushing all over your body, picture a golden band wrapped around your middle. The golden band is warm and comfortable, and it supports and protects your body.

2. Feel the golden band holding you tight and filling you with loving feelings and calmness.

3. Now imagine the golden band has mirrors stuck all around it that face outwards. These mirrors reflect away any spirits you don't wish to talk to. The spirits will understand that you mean them nothing but kindness, but simply do not wish to speak to them at this time.

Part III
Healing and Moving On

Chapter Fifteen:

The Four Steps to Healing

I believe that connecting with the spirits is a valuable part of the grieving process. Learning to hear the spirit of your loved one can offer considerable comfort during times of grief. Furthermore, the spirits can help you make sense of your new world and accept that your loved one has changed form.

I'd like to talk now about healing from grief, and how the spirit world fits in to this process. I will share with you my four steps for healing, and explain how you can use these to help you adjust to the passing of your loved one.

HOW THE SPIRIT REALM HELPS HEALING

If you've lost someone recently, you'll know that nothing is as it was – especially if that person was very close to you. You may be experiencing all sorts of physical and emotional symptoms that feel frightening and strange.

Because we humans have moved away from the intuitive side of life, and embraced only what we can see in the physical realm, death affects most people very strongly. We feel that if someone has left the physical realm, they are gone forever, and our bodies and minds tell us we have 'lost' something.

People often speak of grief as feeling 'empty' and 'hollow', and of course if we are only focusing on the physical realm, the departing of a loved one will indeed leave emptiness.

However, for those of us who have made contact with the spirit realm, death means something different. It *is* an ending of sorts. And yes there *is* emptiness in the material realm where our loved one used to be. But we also understand that where there is emptiness in the physical world, there is fullness and love in spirit.

Our loved one now has a new existence – a timeless existence in a world of love, where there is no pain. This is something to celebrate, especially since one day we will meet them there. We understand that we won't receive their love in the same way as before. But we know that their love is still with us.

As you work through this book and practise your intuitive powers, you will understand and experience the spirit world more and more. You will begin to *know* in your heart and soul that your loved one is there for you, and you will be able to feel them, even though they have left the physical state of being.

The more you make contact with the spirits, the more you will receive help and healing energy from the spiritual realm. Your departed loved one will help you move through grief and adapt to your new life.

THE FOUR STEPS TO HEALING

When we accept the spirit world, we understand that our loved one hasn't disappeared – they have merely changed forms. However, that doesn't mean that their loss from the physical world isn't painful. As human beings, we exist on a physical plane, and many of our senses are designed to recognise the physical world.

To lose the physical presence of a loved one still causes sadness, as we can no longer see, hear and touch them with our physical senses. Until we too are spirits, they are no longer part of the world we inhabit.

In order to accept this major change in our lives, and heal from our sadness, there are four stages of healing that I urge clients to work through.

Read through these stages with me now, and consider how they might fit into your life. We all move through grief at different rates, so not all the stages will be appropriate to you right now. Pick and choose which stages are helpful, and feel free to move through them in any order you wish.

STEP ONE – CELEBRATING YOUR LOVED ONE'S LIFE ON EARTH

Traditionally, we call the celebration of a loved one's life a funeral. Funerals exist in every culture, and are the human way of marking a loved one's passing from one realm to the next.

Many funerals have some religious element, even if the departed soul wasn't religious in their everyday life. I believe this is because death awakens in all of us the understanding that there is more to life than just the physical realm. We understand, because we *feel* our loved one, even though their body has gone, that their spirit must exist somewhere.

Often, funerals are so soon after a death that we haven't had time to accept how our life has changed.

Many clients tell me that they hoped the funeral would give them some sort of closure and acceptance. They hoped that once the 'official' ceremony took place, they would finally get over their shock and understand that their loved one had gone.

In my experience, funerals go some way to helping us accept our loved one's passing, but not all the way. Because they are so soon after the death, we sometimes go through funerals in a state of shock. Part of us can accept that our loved one has changed forms. Another part of us still clings to their physical body, and finds it difficult to accept that they are gone.

I always tell clients that you can have more than one celebration of your loved one's life here on earth. You can celebrate their life every year, or even every month, if you choose.

I believe that the more you celebrate the life of a loved one, the easier it is to accept that their spirit has changed form. I encourage clients to really think about their loved one, the places they liked and their enjoyments here on earth, and hold special parties or gatherings to celebrate their life. You can hold these occasions as many times as you wish.

STEP TWO – LETTING GO OF YOUR LOVED ONE'S PHYSICAL PRESENCE

When our loved one leaves the physical realm, we have to make a lot of adjustments. Yes they are with us and looking over us, but only in spirit. In the physical world, we have to alter our lives to fit around where their physical body once was.

This means accepting the many practical changes you will have to make in the material world, and making some major adjustments. These adjustments can be very painful, but they are less so if you have an understanding of the spirits.

Once we understand that the spirit of our loved one is still very much alive, it becomes easier to deal with the many material objects they left behind.

Clothing, personal possessions and empty homes, rooms or beds may remind us of our loved one's physical presence – but we understand that, in spirit, these items have no value. They only have value to us here on earth. This frees us to choose what to keep and what to discard, without worrying about what our loved one would think if they were alive.

However, just because your loved one is in spirit, and doesn't need material possessions anymore, doesn't mean you have to clear everything out. After all, you still live in the material world, and their old possessions can be a great comfort, and give you wonderful reminders of the physical experiences the two of you shared.

STEP THREE – ALLOW ANY AND ALL FEELINGS TO PASS THROUGH YOU

The passing of a loved one brings with it the need to accept and grow. One of the biggest challenges for my clients is the torrent of emotions that happens after a passing.

Grief is a curious state. It brings with it any and every emotion imaginable, from profound sadness to great joy. I've had clients tell me that they feel angry, relieved, sad, lonely, powerless and frightened, and that these feelings come in a whirlwind, washing around them at all times of day. They never know what they're going to feel from one moment to the next.

This mixture of strong feelings can be extremely difficult to deal with, especially if you're usually quite an even-tempered person.

I always advise clients to let the feelings come. Don't be afraid of them. They are there for a reason.

Accepting your feelings and letting them wash through you is part of the healing process. If you try to hold them up or ignore them, healing will just take longer. I promise that as time goes on, your mind and body will understand that your loved one is in a different realm now. But until then, let your feelings come through. They are there to help you heal.

In spirit, your loved one will help you with these feelings. Just as you're feeling the utmost despair, your loved one will make sure something happens to make you feel loved. Or they will make a difficult task more simple, just when you're at your most tired and in need of help.

Don't discount coincidences that happen when you're working through your feelings. They are your loved one making their presence felt!

Psychic Consultation

A lady called Joy came to see me after the loss of her husband. She told me that before her husband's passing, she'd been a very easy-going type of person, who let her husband arrange everything and never complained.

However, his passing had awakened in her deep feelings of anger and frustration. She was angry at anyone and everyone, for the slightest little thing.

Joy wasn't enjoying this new side of her personality, and hoped that if she could make contact with her husband, she might find a way to make all these feelings 'go away'.

I explained to her that her feelings were perfectly normal, and a natural part of the healing process. They would leave once they had served their purpose.

When we made contact with Joy's husband, he shared how proud he was that she'd arranged the funeral without his help. This, I felt, was his way of helping Joy move into a more independent frame of mind.

The more Joy and I talked, the more we both understood that she was angry at losing her old way of life, and at being forced to be more independent. But she understood that this was necessary now her husband had left the physical world, and that this new way of life would come with tremendous benefits.

STEP FOUR – COMMIT TO GROWTH

Anyone who understands the spirit world knows that death isn't just an ending. It's a beginning too. First, it's a beginning for your departed loved one. They are entering a new and beautiful place, filled with love and happiness. Second, it's a beginning for you. The beginning of your life in the physical realm without your loved one.

In the tarot, many people are scared of the 'death card'. But I always point out that, behind the frightening skull-like figure on a dark horse, there is a bright new dawn. Death is clearing away life, but leaving fertile soil for new things to grow.

Immediately after a passing, most of us are forced to make changes in our lives. These changes may not always be pleasant or welcome. As time passes, we will be met with more choices about life without our loved ones. How will we continue now they are gone? Will we try to cling to our old life, or grow into a new one?

I feel it's vital to *grow* after a passing. If you don't grow, you won't be big enough to accept the loss of your loved one. You will cling to your old life with them in the physical realm, and healing will be stunted.

I recommend taking up new activities, meeting new people (or old ones) and generally pushing your limits and boundaries.

You probably won't feel up to anything like this immediately after a passing, but you will know, as time goes on, that you are ready for growth. You will feel it in your very bones, and your loved one, in spirit, will be guiding you towards people and activities that help you grow.

Some excellent things that can help you grow include: travel, meditation, voluntary work, changing your job and moving house.

You'll know which of these activities feels right to you. If you're really not sure, contact the spirit world and ask your loved one for guidance.

Chapter Sixteen:
The Purpose of Pain

Clients often ask me, 'Why do I have to feel such emotional pain after this loss?' It seems awful that as human beings we have to experience such suffering in our lives, and that much of this suffering comes from losing loved ones.

My response is always the same. Pain has its uses. It forces us to focus on our feelings. It helps us accept change. And it's also a warning system, letting us know when something is wrong, and moving us to make changes in our lives.

Without pain, we would never move on from loss. We'd stay trapped in an old and outdated way of life. So pain is healthy.

This chapter is about how useful pain can be during the grieving process, and how it can help your intuition and your connection with the spirits. We will also talk about how you can use pain to help you move on with your life.

THE BIGGEST WARNING SIGN OF ALL

We all handle grief differently, and feel pain in different ways. However, I have found that grief is always more painful for those who do not have an understanding or awareness of the spirit realm.

As I've just mentioned, pain is a warning system. It tells us something is wrong, and nothing could be more wrong for a human being than losing a loved one and believing they will never see, feel or hear them again.

Those who don't believe in the afterlife are, unfortunately, set to experience the most pain any human being can suffer, and of course this pain is telling them that something is very wrong indeed. The pain is saying they need to open their heart and mind to the intuitive side of life, and feel the spirit of their loved one around them.

I'm not saying for a moment that if you understand the afterlife and feel the spirits, you will not experience pain after loss. We all feel pain as we grow and adjust to our new life without our loved one in the physical realm. However, those who do not believe in the afterlife will be sent a strong, painful signal after a loss. This signal is saying that something is badly wrong. Change the way you are thinking, or you will never feel your loved one's spirit.

HOW PAIN HELPS OUR INTUITION

I believe that severe pain after a loss is designed to put us in touch with our intuition. When we are in deep emotional turmoil, the logical mind shuts down. There simply isn't room for practical, logical thoughts and the emotions take over. Whole days disappear and memories are patchy and built around feelings, rather than words and pictures.

People often speak about being in shock after a loss, and I think this is a good way to describe the intuitive, feeling side of our minds coming to the forefront. The intuition doesn't work on time lines or with labels. It's erratic and creative, and links feelings, colours, pictures and sounds in the strangest combination.

When we are forced into a state of deep feeling, our intuition is heightened and we are very well tuned in to our psychic abilities.

This gives us a better ability to hear and feel the spirit of our loved one, who wants to help soften our loss and our loneliness.

PAIN AND THE POWERFUL PRESENT

Without realising it, many of us spend the day thinking far too much, and imagining the future or the past, rather than living in the present. Pain forces us to appreciate and live in the present moment. When we are feeling pain, we can do nothing but live in the present, and this is very good for us while we are grieving.

Our logical mind thinks about the past and the future, but the intuition works completely in the present – which is why it is such a powerful tool. The mind works on past experiences, but the intuition bases its wisdom on what is *actually* going on *right now*.

If you are thinking of the past or planning the future, you will find it hard to feel your loved ones around you, because they are neither in the past nor the future – they are right here with you now. Pain forces us to live in the present, with the spirits of our loved ones, and helps us feel their loving energy at the time when we need it most.

PAIN AND CHANGE

One of the key reasons we feel pain when we grieve is because this forces us to make the necessary changes in our lives that result from the loss of a loved one.

Pain lets us know something is wrong, and when we have lost someone, there will be many, many practical elements in our lives that no longer work.

If you have lost a partner, your home may no longer be suitable for you now you are living alone. If you used to phone your mother every weekend for a long chat, but now she is gone, your weekends need to be rethought.

Basically, pain tells us that life can't be the same. It has to change. By making us feel uncomfortable, it forces us to make the changes that otherwise we might not make.

It we didn't feel pain after a loss, we may carry on living our old life as if our loved one were still in it, and this would do us no good at all. Pain says, 'you have to change something, otherwise I'm going to make you feel uncomfortable'. And change we do. Slowly but surely. And the more we change and move away from our old life and accept a new one, the duller our pain becomes.

EMOTIONS AND THE BODY

The mind and the body are very powerfully linked, and the more you connect with your intuition and psychic energy, the more you will feel this to be true. What hurts the mind can hurt the body, and vice versa.

Emotional pain is there for a reason. If we do not accept emotional pain, or try to ignore it by distracting ourselves with work or constant thinking, the pain will almost certainly transfer to our body, where it can cause long-term damage.

This is why it is so important to accept and acknowledge pain, and also to respond to it. Pain wants us to take action. It wants us to make changes in our lives, and also to connect deeply with our emotions and pay attention to our intuition. If we don't take action when we are in emotional pain, and make major changes in our lives, then our bodies will suffer.

If you have any aches and pains that seem to have come out of nowhere, think carefully about how they may be linked with emotional pain. Did they come at a time of great emotional pain or stress? Are they in key emotional centres of the body, such as the heart, intestines or chest?

If you suspect that you're holding emotional pain in the body, it's very important to recognise which emotion is linked to this pain. You can do this by talking with others, connecting with your intuition and your loved one, and also by *expressing* your emotional pain. Let's talk about that now.

LETTING PAIN OUT

We all have to experience some degree of pain when we lose a loved one. It is life's way of helping our intuition, and forcing us to make changes. However, that doesn't mean you have to suffer quietly. I believe it's very healthy to express your pain, as long as you don't hurt others when you do so. As a matter of fact, if you don't express your pain in a healthy, truthful way, the chances are you *will* end up hurting others at some point, as your pent-up feelings will turn into anger and aggression. Or they will become physical ailments in the body.

Let's look at some of the ways you can express grief pains.

Talking to friends and relatives

It's very important that while you're grieving you are able to express how you feel to at least one friend or relative. You need to be able to share, at any given time, exactly how you're feeling, even if you're ashamed or embarrassed by those feelings.

I've had clients who have felt all sorts of ugly feelings.

Ideally, this friend or relative will have lost someone too, or be grieving the same loss as yourself.

Trust is the key, as when we grieve, we can experience some very odd and uncomfortable feelings, and indeed feelings that perhaps don't show us in a very favourable light. You need to be able to trust that whoever you talk to won't judge you or think of you differently, and will understand just how tumultuous the grieving process can be.

I've had clients who have felt all sorts of ugly feelings, from jealousy towards other relatives to anger at not receiving a fair cut of the will. Some clients have even felt hatred towards the person who died.

Sometimes death reveals family secrets too, and things that some people would either rather not know, or rather not have aired in public.

Find a friend or relative with whom you can confess your ugliest feelings, and you will have found a very healthy release for the pain of the grieving process.

Shouting and screaming

You may be a little surprised to see this heading, but no – you haven't read it wrong! I think having a good shout and a scream is a very healthy way to express pain. Of course, you have to find somewhere quiet and private to do it, as you don't want to upset anyone. I like to have a good shout and scream in my car on the motorway, where no one can see or hear me.

Feel free to shout whatever you want. Don't censor yourself or be ashamed or embarrassed by what comes out of your mouth. Just let it come out, and know it's healthy to express it.

Exercise

Doing some fast-paced exercise, such as jogging, dancing or even jumping up and down on the spot, can help you let go of pent-up emotions – especially the ones you hold in your chest. You could also consider finding a punch bag and pounding the living daylights out of it – a great way to express your pain!

Counselling

I recommend that anyone who has lost someone close to them seeks counselling as a way to express their pain. A counsellor is trained to help you express yourself, without judging or giving advice. He or she will provide a safe environment for you to express your pain and also to discover how you're truly feeling. Friends and relatives can be great to talk to, but counsellors are trained in helping you bring feelings out, and expressing every last bit of pain. Your doctor will be able to recommend a good grief counsellor in your area.

Psychic Consultation

A gentleman called Doug came to see me not long after the loss of his adult son. Everything about his face and body told me he was in absolute anguish. His son had died of an unexplained illness, and neither the hospital nor any of the doctors whom Doug had seen really understood why he had passed.

Doug felt very strongly that he needed an explanation for his son's sudden passing, and had come to me in the hope that the spirits would provide him with one.

Doug was clearly suffering a whole range of painful emotions, but when I asked him how he was feeling, he could only say that he felt numb. I have to say that men are much worse at expressing their feelings than women – which isn't really their fault, since most men are told to be the 'tough guy' all their lives.

I told Doug that until he connected with his feelings, we might experience a blocked path to the spirit realm. We spoke for a while about the way in which Doug's son passed, and I listened and focused on how this made Doug feel.

After twenty minutes or so, Doug stopped talking about doctors and medicine, and started talking my language – the language of feelings. The change in him was instant. The pain that was set in his face loosened as he spoke of his deep feelings of guilt and inferiority whenever he was in the hospital with his son. As a 'normal working man', he didn't feel he knew enough about medicine to help his son, and felt he was somehow to blame for his son's death.

In truth, he was visiting me to lay his guilt to rest.

We connected with Doug's son, Jamie, and as I suspected Jamie wasn't interested in talking about his old physical life or his body. Instead he asked his father to talk more with his mother, so they could work through their grief together.

Now that Doug had listened to his feelings, he left my session a much lighter man. I knew he had a journey ahead of him, as he'd have many more feelings to work through, but at least he was on the right path.

Chapter Seventeen:

How the Spirits Help Us Heal

The spirits don't have to come through and talk to us. They *choose* to come through, and I believe they do this, in part, to help us heal. Connecting with the spirits is a very great comfort when we have lost someone dear, and can help us through the tough grieving process.

I'm going to talk now about the different ways the spirits help us heal. We will also look at some of the things you may experience as you grieve, that will show you the spirits are around and looking after you.

HOW THE SPIRITS EASE LONELINESS

When we lose someone close, it's very common to feel lonely almost immediately after the loss. Where our loved one used to be, filling the physical world with warmth and energy, there is now an empty space.

If we've lost someone who lived with us, the sense of loneliness can be even more profound. Loneliness can be one of the most painful parts of grief, but it's something the spirits are constantly trying to help us through.

> *It's common for people to try and distract themselves from their feelings after the loss of a loved one.*

Many clients come to see me because they are lonely, and because they want to feel once more the warm energy of their departed loved one. I am always delighted to share their loved one's energy with them, and also to explain that this loving energy is all around them, all the time, if only they know how to look for it.

The spirits *want* us to know that we're not alone, and they are trying to show us all the time that they are there – especially when we feel lonely. The trouble is, in our busy logical lives, we often don't *feel* what they are trying to share, because we are too busy thinking, planning and distracting ourselves.

The spirits will help you through loneliness and keep you company always, but you have to be tuned in to your feelings and intuition to sense that they are there. This can take courage, as our feelings can be very painful while we grieve.

It's common for people to try and distract themselves from their feelings after the loss of a loved one. Many of my clients tell me they watch endless television, or busy themselves with work or activities so they don't have time to think about their loss. Others tell me they take sleeping tablets or antidepressants to numb the pain.

Simply feel what you need to feel.

I know just how painful and gruelling grief can be, and I don't judge anyone for trying to cope however they see fit. But the truth is, it's much harder to hear the spirits if you're distracting yourself, or numbing your pain with medication. The spirits will keep you company and banish loneliness, but only if you're able fully to tune in to your feelings.

Do you distract yourself from your grief by giving yourself lots of tasks to do? Do you take medication or drink alcohol to help numb your feelings? If you do, the chances are you are cutting yourself off from a great source of company, because you will find it hard to feel the spirits around you.

It's fine to distract yourself sometimes, but if you're on a mission to sidestep the painful feelings of grief, then I would urge you to take an hour of quiet time and really experience the companionship the spirits have to offer. Yes – you will most likely feel pain during this process. It *is* painful to realise that your loved one is no longer in this realm with you. But your loved one will quietly keep you company through this pain, and help you feel less lonely.

During your hour with your loved one, don't look at the television or computer. Turn off your phone. Don't allow yourself to be distracted by jobs around the house. Simply feel what you need to feel, and I guarantee that alongside those feelings of pain and loss, you will experience a profound love that will ease feelings of loneliness.

HEALING THE FEAR OF DEATH

When we lose a loved one, we often start thinking about our own life and death. We realise that our time in the physical world won't last forever, and many of us can develop a real fear of illness and dying.

Nursing a loved one through an illness and seeing the physical body decay can be traumatising, and awaken fears of physical pain and suffering, and of course death.

This can be especially true if a parent has passed, as we link ourselves to our parents, and feel that their illnesses may be our illnesses.

Knowing that there is an afterlife and that it is a wonderful place is very great comfort to anyone who fears dying.

Sometimes, this can have a positive outcome. Many of my clients have changed their lifestyles for the better following the death of a loved one. I remember very well one gentleman whose father died of lung cancer at the age of fifty. The gentleman immediately gave up smoking, and committed to more exercise and a healthier lifestyle.

It's wonderful to live a healthier life, but you shouldn't fear death.

When you have an understanding of the spirit world and are able to connect regularly, you will see that death is nothing to be afraid of. In fact, there's really no such thing as death since our spirits live on eternally.

Knowing that there is an afterlife and that it is a wonderful place is very great comfort to anyone who fears dying. Best of all, the spirits want us to know how happy they are, and that they haven't truly left existence.

If you find yourself dwelling on death or illness, and fearing your own death, I'd urge you to connect with the spirits as often as you can. They will reassure you that not only is there life after death, but that it is a good, happy life that is peaceful and free of pain. They want you to enjoy the rest of your time on earth without worrying about dying, but they are also ready to welcome you to the spirit realm when you pass.

HEALING COINCIDENCES

When you lose a loved one, you'll start to see coincidences. These will probably seem to occur most often immediately after a passing. Perhaps you'll be searching for a special piece of music for the funeral, and suddenly a forgotten favourite record appears. Or just when you're feeling at a low ebb, a close friend or relative will call to see how you're doing.

These coincidences are the spirits taking care of you and helping you heal. Although coincidences may *seem* to appear immediately after a passing, the truth is they happen all the time. You're just more likely to notice them when a loss is recent, and your loved one is constantly on your mind.

Coincidences are one of the ways the spirit of your loved one will show you that they are still around, taking care of you and offering a helping hand. Love never dies, it only changes. In life, your loved one could show you love by talking to you and touching you. Now they have passed, they have a new way of doing things. They help you heal from grief by giving you a little helping hand every so often.

Even those who don't believe in the spirits will experience coincidences, and it always makes me smile to hear stories of the 'lucky things' that happen following a passing. I know that these 'lucky things' are the spirits showing their love.

Let me share with you now coincidences experienced by two of my clients.

A lady who lost her husband was scared witless at the thought of having to sell her family home. She'd never dealt with solicitors or estate agents before, and was terrified that she'd get everything wrong and end up hugely out of pocket.

She knew she had to sell quickly as bills were mounting up, but she'd been putting off the process since her husband's passing.

> *Clients have told me about all sorts of coincidences that happened after a passing.*

Three months after her husband's funeral, she received some huge bills that she knew she'd struggle to pay. Alongside the bills was a card for a local estate agent.

Knowing she had to sell quickly, the lady called the estate

agent and was delighted to discover that the head of the agency was an old friend of her husband's.

Not only did this gentleman guide her through the whole process, he ensured that she got the very best deal for her home, arranged good solicitors and waived the estate agent fees. He told her it was the least he could do for the wife of his old friend.

Another client of mine lost his father suddenly and had no money for the funeral. He was very upset at the thought that he might not be able to give his father a good sendoff, and started applying for loans and credit cards – even though he'd only just paid off a long-standing debt and was getting his financial life back on track.

When he visited the funeral home to get costs for his father's ceremony and cremation, the lady there noticed how distressed he was about the money side of things, and told him about a local charity that helped with funeral expenses. The local charity was happy to help this gentleman pay for his father's funeral, saving him much anguish.

Clients have told me about all sorts of coincidences that happened after a passing. Brochures appearing in strange places, phone calls just when they're needed and helpful television or radio programmes cropping up to guide them into their new life. These coincidences are the spirits showing their love and helping us heal.

THE SPIRITS AND PHYSICAL HEALING

The spirits will help you through emotional pain, especially feelings of grief. However, many people don't realise that the spirits can also help heal physical pain. I believe that most physical pain is caused by pent-up emotions and, for this reason, you are much more likely to suffer aches and pains during times of grief.

We have so many feelings whirling around when we grieve,

but the world we live in tells us it's not appropriate to show them. We're allowed to cry and wail at funerals, but other than that we're supposed to keep our feelings in check when we're at work or in company.

I believe these pent-up feelings can lead to physical ailments such as bad backs, headaches, colds, stomach bugs and digestive complaints.

The spirits can help heal the physical body if you let them. As with most things in life, it's simply a question of asking. If you have some pain in your body, take the time to relax and steady your breathing, then ask the spirits to help heal your pain.

You may find that the pain clears up very quickly, or that some sort of answer will drop into your head about how the pain can be resolved. You may hear the spirits urging you to have a good cry, or to tell a family member how you truly feel. Often, the spirits will simply find a way for you to rest and take care of yourself. A fully scheduled day may suddenly, and oddly, be cancelled, so that you find yourself with time to rest and recuperate. Don't discount coincidences like these – they're the spirits at work.

The spirits know that life will never be the same for us, now they have left the physical realm. And they want to help us to accept this fact, and build a new life without them in it. They will give us strength and courage, just when we think we're at our lowest ebb and can't cope with life anymore.

At low moments, the spirits will fill you with love and help pick you up. They may do this be sending a friend or relative to give you support. Or they may simply give you the feeling, out of nowhere, that YES, you can do this and you are strong enough to get through.

Be assured that no matter how hard you are grieving, you have a wealth of love and support out there to help you. Grief is a long journey, but with the spirits around you, you will heal.

Chapter Eighteen:

Finding Your Spirit Guide

As you become more experienced at contacting the spirits, you will begin to understand that there are many spirits out there who want to guide you in life and pick you up when you are down.

These are often the spirits of people you never met in life, but who have a special attraction to you and have the particular wisdom that can help you on life's journey.

This chapter is about finding these 'spirit guides', and connecting with them for a lifetime of support and wisdom.

You will instinctively know when you meet a spirit who wants to be your guide, and the connection between the two of you will help you a great deal in life.

THE DIFFERENCE BETWEEN DEPARTED LOVED ONES AND SPIRIT GUIDES

You may be feeling a little confused by this chapter. After all, isn't a departed loved one a spirit guide? Aren't they one and the same thing? Well, not quite. Of course, your departed loved one is watching over you and offering you guidance. They are sharing their love with you and helping you in life, even at times when you're not aware of them. You have a deep and loving connection with the spirit of your departed loved one, because you knew them in life. The two of you have a bond that can never be broken, even though you are now living in two different realms.

Your spirit guide, on the other hand, has probably never met you in this realm. In fact, they may not even have lived in the physical realm. If they have done, they may have had many different physical lives.

It's very exciting to meet the spirits who have a connection with us and want to guide us through life.

Spirit guides are 'experienced' spirits – ones who have been in the afterlife for a long time, and have never-ending wisdom and love. They are highly mature spirits who take care of others in both the afterlife and the physical realm.

Sometimes, spirit guides are family members whom we haven't met in life. For example, great, great grandparents or very distant relatives from hundreds of years ago. However, I find this is the exception rather than the rule.

We all have dozens of spirit guides, but if we're to meet them and feel their presence, we have to take the time to meditate and bring them to us. It's very exciting to meet the spirits who have a connection with us and want to guide us through life. What will they look like? What will their personality be like?

Every spirit guide is different, and since they are 'old souls' you will experience deep feelings of love and wisdom when you connect with them. Their messages will usually come through loud and clear.

Your departed loved ones, on the other hand, are 'new souls' in the afterlife. They will not be as experienced at making the connection between their world and ours, and therefore won't always come through clearly when you try to connect. They are still around you, though, and always sending love.

HOW SPIRIT GUIDES CAN HELP US CONNECT

Because our spirit guides are 'old souls', they are experts at bridging the gap between the afterlife and the physical realm. This means that they come through all the time to try and share wisdom with us.

Spirit guides are so good at connecting with the physical realm that they often come through *before* the spirit of our loved ones. They will then help find our loved one's spirit in the afterlife, and if the connection is a little shaky, they will try to strengthen it.

As soon as you ask, the heavens will bend to try to give you what you require.

If I'm ever having trouble making a connection, I often call upon my spirit guide to help me. I can usually hear my guide fairly clearly, even if the connection to the spirit world is a little bit wobbly. My guide will let me know if a spirit doesn't want to come through right now, or if another spirit is shouting louder and has important information to share.

If you need your spirit guide's help when making a connection, simply ASK. It's as simple as that. We so rarely ask for things in life, but one of the key things I've learned about the spirit world is that you can and must ask for whatever you need. As soon as you ask, the heavens will bend to try to give you what you require.

MEETING YOUR SPIRIT GUIDES

I wonder who your spirit guides will be? Perhaps you already have an idea or a feeling. I have a wonderful exercise that will help you bring your spirit guides forward, so you can start building a lifelong connection of wisdom and learning.

Calling Forth Your Guide Exercise

We all have many, many spirit guides, but (especially for beginners) I'd advise you to try to meet one at a time, otherwise things can get a little confusing.

Before calling forth your guide, I'd like you to dress in your favourite clothes — the outfit that makes you feel most like you. This may be a dressy outfit, or something casual. It's totally up to you. Whatever reflects you the best.

Now go to a personal space — somewhere that is yours and yours alone. Ideally this will be a bedroom or personal study room.

If you like, you can play a little of your favourite music to warm the spirits and get good vibrations going.

Now turn off any music and begin meditation. Take in long, slow deep breaths, in through the nose, out through the mouth.

Breathe slowly and deeply like this for at least ten minutes, until you can feel your thoughts drifting away and your feelings and intuition begin to take over.

Allow your imagination to place you on top of a mountain. The air is cool and clear, and a bright sun shines overhead. It's not too hot or cold. Beneath your feet, you can feel solid, craggy rock and you can see a path winding down the mountain.

However, you can only see a little of the path, because beneath you the mountain is surrounded by cloud.

Watch the path.

Now. Say out loud: 'I call upon my spirit guide to come forwards'.

It's a wonderful thing to feel even a single spirit guide in your life.

Through the cloud, your spirit guide will walk towards you. Keep an open mind, and welcome whoever comes. It could be someone young or old, or even an animal. You may not see anything, but simply feel the cloud clearing and get a strong sense of a personality — perhaps someone witty and funny or calm and wise.

Let your spirit guide come forwards and welcome them into your life. Tell them that you're looking forward to receiving their wisdom.

Once you have met one of your guides (remember – you have many!), you will feel their energy often. Sometimes you will hear them laughing with joy when you make a good decision, or you may hear words of caution if you're about to take a wrong turn.

It's a wonderful thing to feel even a single spirit guide in your life. Not only will they enrich your life with their wisdom, they will strengthen your connection to your loved ones in spirit and help you make connections for others.

DIFFERENT GUIDES AT DIFFERENT TIMES

At different times in our lives, different spirit guides will come forwards to help us. You will probably have one main guide – the spirit you first met on top of the mountain – but you should also be open to a wealth of other personalities coming forwards to help you in life.

For example, there are healing guides who are particularly good during times of illness and physical pain. These guides are able to go within your body, and the bodies of others, and help release the emotions that you are holding in your physical self.

Many people see their healing guides as doctors or nurses, and indeed I believe that many healing guides were once medical people in the physical realm. A friend of mine is guided by a Roman doctor who has so far cured her of many pains and ailments!

You will also meet learning guides, who help you soak up knowledge or find just the right bit of information that you are looking for. These people were often teachers or spiritual leaders if they ever lived on earth.

All sorts of guides will come forwards for you, the more you listen to your feelings and intuition, and really open yourself up to the wisdom and assistance of the spirits.

SPIRIT GUIDES AND GRIEF

The 'old souls' who become spirit guides pay particular attention to us when we're grieving. They understand that we need their help more than ever during times of grief, and that we're especially open to the connections between their world and our own after we lose a loved one.

The mission of spirit guides is to help us understand that there is life after death, and that the loss of your loved one in this life isn't an ending.

Spirit guides are full of sadness for anyone who doesn't believe in life after death. They know that if a person truly believes a loved one is gone forever, they will experience the most extreme pain and suffering known to man. They don't want anyone to suffer in this way, and spend much of their time helping grieving people see and feel their loved ones in the afterlife.

You will understand yourself, during your journey to connect with the afterlife, that it is a very great comfort to know your loved one is nearby. Spirit guides are heartbroken for anyone who doesn't feel this connection, and work hard to help bridge the gap between this world and the next.

Psychic Consultation

An elderly lady came to see me after the death of her mother. This lady was herself in her early seventies, but her dear old mother had lived to ninety-six years of age.

The lady, whose name was Erica, had no doubt whatsoever that her mother was still around, and took very great comfort in this fact. However, she also had the sense of another presence when she thought of her mother – a smiling young lad, who wore a peaked cap and had smudges of coal on his face.

She was baffled by this image, and wondered if I could explain where this boy had come from. Had her mother had another child, she wanted to know? She was certain she'd never met this lad in life, and he didn't look at all like her father, who'd departed many years ago.

I explained that, despite his young age, this boy was actually a very mature spirit and was here to guide her. He was her spirit guide, and was coming through very strongly now that she was opening herself up to thoughts of the afterlife.

A slow smile spread over Erica's face when I said this, and she nodded in understanding.

'Yes,' she said. 'Now that you've said that, I know you're right. He looks like a lad, but he doesn't seem like a lad at all. There's something about his expression that tells me he's been around a long time, and is far wiser than I am.'

Erica was delighted to have met one of her spirit guides, and asked me how she could connect with him regularly. I told her she probably wouldn't have to try too hard, since she'd found him already. Once we see or feel one of our guides, they usually find it very easy to come through often and send us wisdom.

Chapter Nineteen:
Channelling the Spirits for Others

The more you get the hang of connecting with the spirit world and drawing your loved ones to you, the more all sorts of spirits will try to use you as their voice. There is nothing to be afraid of when this happens. Indeed, it is a sign that your intuition has become very strong indeed, and the spirits are supporting you more than ever.

When unfamiliar spirits make contact, their messages can be a little hard to interpret at first. However, with practice you will hear them just as clearly as the voices of your loved ones.

If you are hearing the voices of unfamiliar spirits, I believe it is time to start sharing your gift and reading for others. This chapter will tell you how to do just that, and also how to start working as a professional medium, if you feel this is your destiny.

HEARING UNFAMILIAR SPIRITS

When you first start hearing unfamiliar spirits, you may not be sure that the strange images you're seeing or words you're hearing belong to the afterlife. You may just put them down to your imagination, and focus even harder on connecting with your loved one. But as time goes on, the words and images of unfamiliar spirits will grow clearer, and you will have a definite sense of their personalities. If they were ever alive on the earthly plane, you may get a picture of what they used to look like.

You should never be afraid of any spirits, even if they're completely unfamiliar. All spirits are loving, caring creatures and will fill you with a sense of peace and calm when they come through. If you're not feeling peace and calm, then you're not connected with a spirit.

If an unfamiliar spirit comes through while you're trying to connect with a loved one, I'd advise that you take some time to listen to what this new spirit has to say. They may have an important message for you or someone close to you.

However, if you'd rather not hear another spirit, you can simply ask them to leave and they will.

You needn't ever feel bad about asking a spirit to step back from a connection. In fact, it's very important that you *are* able to tell certain spirits 'not now' once you start reading for other people. You will at times find yourself overwhelmed by many different spirits, and you'll need to carefully direct who comes forward and who steps back.

Directing the spirits is a very important skill when it comes to reading for others. Let's talk about that now.

DIRECTING THE SPIRITS

When you begin reading for yourself, the chances are you'll struggle even to bring your loved one through. However, as your experience grows, you are likely to hear several different spirits at once, often at times when you haven't consciously connected to the afterlife.

The spirits may come to you in dreams, or when you're just about to fall asleep or have just woken up. They can even come to you on the bus on the way to work!

It's a beautiful thing to hear the voices of many spirits, but if you're reading for others you need to be able to direct who comes forwards and who steps back.

Once you've asked the spirits to come forwards, tell them who you have with you and ask if anyone has a message for that person. Then let your intuition seek out the right spirit. Don't look too closely or try too hard. Just let your mind drift around the spirits until someone or something glows. Focus on the glow and energy, and watch as that spirit comes forwards.

If any other spirits who don't have that glow or energy try to come forwards, just tell them politely to step back and that you don't need them at this time. I promise they will understand.

READING FOR FRIENDS

As a beginner, I'd strongly recommend you read for people you know first and foremost. It's much easier to understand spirit messages for people you know, and friends will be more understanding if you can't connect, or if the messages are foggy and don't make sense.

Find a friend who is like-minded and wants to connect with the spirit world. Then arrange a quiet hour or so for the two of you in one of your homes, and spend some time making yourself calm, breathing deeply and surrounding yourself with white light – just as you'd do if you were reading for yourself.

It is a privilege to be able to share love from the spirit world, and reassure others that their departed are happy and at peace.

You may find that, just like when you first tried to connect for yourself, nothing comes and your first session is a little disappointing. That's why it's good to be with a friend at first, who will understand that you're learning and forgive you for not getting it right first time.

After three or four sessions, you will find that images and pictures do start to come through. Most likely, your own loved one's spirit will come through first, and this is fine. It shows the connection is open. Then your loved one will bring through the spirit you are looking for, or simply hold the connection open so others can come through.

The first time you successfully manage to bring through a spirit for another person is very exciting. It is a privilege to be able to share love from the spirit world, and reassure others that their departed are happy and at peace.

I'd recommend working with the same friend for a little while – at least a few months – until you can very quickly and easily bring their departed loved one through. Give yourself plenty of time and be patient. It will take as long as it takes.

READING FOR NEW PEOPLE

Once you've practised reading for friends, you may decide that you'd like to share your gift with others. Indeed, you may find that people you've never met, or hardly know, seek you out when they hear that you can connect with the spirits.

It's a wonderful thing to bring love from the spirits to as many people as possible, and I would urge you to read for others as often as you can. However, when you read for strangers, I'd advise arranging things more professionally, to ensure the person you're reading for is relaxed and calm. Friends will generally be relaxed in your company anyway, but a stranger may not be, and this can create a block to the spirits.

Your first job with a stranger is to put them at ease, and one of the first ways you do this is by creating the right environment. It's nice to read in your own home, but I'd recommend arranging the room you read in so that it's a little less personal than usual. You're looking to create a neutral space where anyone would feel at home, so remove books, clutter and personal possessions. You may also want to warm some lemon oil, or similar fragrance, to create a neutral, clean aroma.

Ask the person what area of their life they'd like to cover, and if they have any fears about making contact.

If the person you're reading for is a total stranger, ask someone else to be in the house (but out of the way) so you can feel safe.

Make sure there is a clean and comfortable place for each of you to sit, and ideally place the person so they are facing the door. It's best if the two of you sit at right angles to each other, so you are neither directly facing (which can be intimidating) nor side by side.

If you will be using cards and a table for your reading, make sure it is clean and covered with a nice, neutral-coloured cloth.

Start the session by asking if the person you're with has ever had a reading before. If they haven't, explain that there is no such thing as a bad spirit, and that all the spirits want to do is share their love with us. If they have previously had a reading, ask about their experience. Contrary to popular belief, most experiences with mediums are positive, but if they have had a negative experience, reassure them that today is going to be nothing but good.

You will then want to explain how you personally connect with the spirits, and what they can expect from the session.

Ask the person what area of their life they'd like to cover, and if they have any fears about making contact. If they do have fears, tell them that the spirits have only love for us, and they have nothing to fear. Ask them to take some deep breaths with you to calm down.

When you connect, be mindful that the person you are with may be impatient to hear messages, and try to hold off telling them what you are hearing and seeing until the messages are very clear.

At the end of the session, talk to the person about how they are feeling. Bear in mind that we can feel all sorts of things after connecting with a loved one, from gentle sadness to great joy. However, overall a connection should be an uplifting experience. It should revive us and help us through any difficult times that lie ahead.

WORKING AS A PROFESSIONAL MEDIUM

The more you connect for others, the more you are likely to consider turning your hand to professional mediumship. Some people don't like the idea of charging money for mediumship, but I think it's perfectly okay. Money is simply energy, and it takes a lot of energy to connect to the spirit world. If you have spent many months and years developing your intuition and your talent, there is no reason why you should not be paid for your time when you connect for others.

If you connect often and don't charge, your energy levels will be depleted. However, if you take money for your services, you can then use this money energy to pay for things that save you time, and also to advertise your services more widely to others.

The more people you can connect for and help through their grief, the better the world will be. It is perfectly right that your energy is replaced with money energy for providing this service.

How do you know that you're ready to become a professional medium? Well, first you'll have the *desire* to spend a good deal of your time connecting for others. Some of us have this desire, some of us don't. If you only ever want to connect for yourself or close friends, that is absolutely fine. However, if you do desire to connect for strangers on a regular basis, you should certainly put a price on your time, and by doing this you are moving into the world of professional mediumship.

The saying goes that when the student is ready, the teacher will appear.

The second way you'll know you're ready to become a professional medium is simply this: a teacher will appear to guide you through the process. Every professional medium is a novice when he or she starts out, and every one of us needs a good teacher. The saying goes that when the student is ready, the teacher will appear, and this is very true of professional mediumship.

You may meet your teacher through friends of friends, or stumble across some sort of training course on the internet. You may visit a favourite medium yourself, and discover that she has just started offering tuition. However it happens, you will find you don't have to try very hard to find a teacher when the time is right.

If you decide to offer your services professionally, you will find a large network of like-minded and supportive people who will help you on your journey. Good mediums are not the least bit competitive. Our aim is to help as many people as possible feel the love of the spirits, and as far as we're concerned, the more mediums around the better.

Psychic Consultation

For many years, I read for a friend of mine called Rachel, and helped bring through the spirit of her brother. Rachel was always very interested in the spirit world, and keen to develop her own intuition, so we went to meditation together, and I talked her through how she could connect by herself.

It took a few months, but eventually Rachel was able to connect to her brother's spirit on her own, and after a year, she began hearing the spirits of people she'd never met before.

Excited by her growing intuition, Rachel began reading for friends and eventually strangers. After her hundredth reading, she decided it was time to share her gift with even more people, and become a professional medium.

On the exact day Rachel made this decision, an email arrived from one of the spiritual groups she'd joined. It offered a mediumship course taught by a male medium whom Rachel had very much admired over the years.

Rachel signed up for the course and never looked back. She learned everything she needed to learn, and enjoyed her time with a great teacher. Now she reads part-time for others, and hosts séances at a local spiritualist church. She loves working as a medium, although, as she says, it doesn't really feel like work at all.

Chapter Twenty:

Moving On with Your Life

I believe that the spirits connect with this world in order to help us move on with our lives. The spirits have no physical body and no desire to return to the earthly realm. However, they understand that now they are gone, we have a lot of changes to go through, and they want to help us with these changes.

As time goes on and grief heals, you will find your connection with the spirit world changes – or at least, it *should* change. This final chapter is about what happens to your connection with the spirits as you move on with your life, and how to keep their love around you at all times.

CONNECTING LESS OFTEN AS TIME GOES ON

Clients often ask me how often they should connect with the spirits, and whether it's unhealthy to connect too often. In the early days of grief, there is a strong desire to connect as often as possible, and I feel this is perfectly healthy. Of course you want the love and advice of your lost loved one. The spirit of your loved one wants to give you support and ease your loneliness, and I feel there is no harm at all in connecting whenever you choose to in the early days.

However, as time goes on, life should go on too. If a year has passed since the loss of your loved one, and you still feel a desire to connect very regularly, the spirits will start sending you messages that indicate it's time to make changes.

> *You will join the afterlife one day, but until that day comes*
> *there are many wonderful, rich and fulfilling days ahead of you*
> *in the material realm.*

You may find your connection growing fuzzy every so often, or you may regularly hear the spirits urging you to make new friends, change your lifestyle or move house. You may find that just when you'd found a quiet space and time to connect, something happens that means you have to postpone making contact. Perhaps an urgent phone call will come through, or there'll be a knock at the door.

The spirits only want what's best for you, and what's best for you is to *truly* live in this world while you're in it. If you spend too much time trying to connect with the afterlife, you are missing life here on earth, and the spirits don't want that.

You will join the afterlife one day, but until that day comes there are many wonderful, rich and fulfilling days ahead of you in the material realm. The spirits don't want you to miss out on them. Remember that, much as the spirits are there to love and support you, they also want you to rebuild your life and not rely on them too much for companionship.

It's healthy to connect less often with the spirit world as time goes by and your loved one's passing is less raw. Don't feel that you are neglecting the spirits, or that they'll miss you. They won't. On the contrary – they are happy that you are living fully in this life, and looking forward to seeing you in the next.

If you find you've got yourself into something of a habit of connecting, and wish to connect less often, I'd recommend that you ask the spirits to change the way they communicate with you. Connect with them, as you usually would, and tell them that you'd like to feel them around you on a day-to-day basis. Then don't connect for a while, and see what happens. Most likely, you'll experience a series of coincidences that tell you your loved ones are there and looking after you.

LOVE OVER TIME

As time goes on and your grief heals, you will find that not only will you connect less often with the spirit world, but that your reasons for connecting will change.

Whereas at first you will tend to look for relief from the raw pain of grief, as time goes on your feelings will be softer. You will still enjoy the love and companionship the spirits have to offer, but you will be more interested in finding answers to questions and queries, and getting help to make difficult decisions.

Instead of desperately seeking a connection, you will find that you are much more able to let messages come as and when they are ready to.

As you move further away from a passing, you will feel the love of the spirits around you more and more, and in turn you will connect less often. In the long term, this is a much gentler and less consuming way to live.

The spirits are around us at all times, and see and hear everything. They know our deepest troubles and fears, and do everything they can to help us live a happy and fulfilling life. Once you know this, life is better.

I always say that I've never really lost anyone I cared about. I just can't see them anymore. And I'm sure in your heart, you know this to be true, too.

I sincerely hope you've enjoyed this journey with me into the spirit world, and that you've felt all the love that comes from knowing the spirits are all around you.

With light and love, I wish you a happy life and I hope to meet you one day, in this world or the next.

Index